Introduction to Automotive Cybersecurity

Introduction

Historical context

In today's fast-paced, interconnected world, the automotive industry stands at the forefront of technological innovation. Modern vehicles are no longer just mechanical marvels; they have evolved into rolling computers on wheels. This transformation has not only revolutionized the driving experience but has also introduced new challenges and vulnerabilities, chief among them being automotive cybersecurity.

To appreciate the significance of automotive cybersecurity, one must delve into its historical context. Understanding how we arrived at this juncture is essential in navigating the complexities of safeguarding vehicles against digital threats.

The Mechanical Era

The roots of the automotive industry trace back to the late 19th century, with pioneers like Karl Benz and Henry Ford introducing the world to the marvels of the motor vehicle. In these early days, cars were purely mechanical contraptions, devoid of any digital components. The idea of a "car hack" was inconceivable as there were no computers or electronic control units (ECUs) to compromise.

The Emergence of Digital Control

The 20th century brought about a pivotal shift as automotive engineers began incorporating electronic systems for improved performance, safety, and comfort. The introduction of the Engine Control Unit (ECU) marked a significant milestone. ECUs allowed for more precise control over engine functions, optimizing fuel efficiency and emissions.

As digital technology became more pervasive, ECUs multiplied and evolved to control various aspects of the vehicle, from anti-lock brakes to airbags. Vehicles were becoming increasingly reliant on software and electronic components. This shift enhanced vehicle performance and opened the door to exciting new features, but it also laid the groundwork for cybersecurity concerns.

The First Signs of Vulnerability

In the early 21st century, automotive cybersecurity entered the public consciousness. Researchers began uncovering vulnerabilities in vehicles' digital systems. The emergence of keyless entry systems and wireless tire pressure monitoring systems raised concerns. These convenience features, while enhancing the driving experience, also presented opportunities for malicious actors to exploit wireless communications.

In 2010, researchers demonstrated the remote hijacking of a car's systems, a watershed moment that alerted the industry to the looming threats. It was a wake-up call for manufacturers to recognize that cars, like any other connected devices, could be hacked.

Industry Response and Regulations

As the threat landscape evolved, the automotive industry mobilized to address cybersecurity concerns. Manufacturers started implementing security measures in their vehicles, and organizations such as the Society of Automotive Engineers (SAE) began developing standards for automotive cybersecurity. These standards aimed to guide manufacturers in securing their vehicles against potential threats.

Furthermore, governments around the world recognized the importance of regulating the automotive cybersecurity domain. Laws like the U.S. SPY Car Act and the EU's General Data Protection Regulation (GDPR) extended their reach to include the automotive sector, emphasizing the need for safeguarding personal data and ensuring the integrity of vehicle systems.

High-Profile Incidents

The journey of automotive cybersecurity is also marked by high-profile incidents that captured public attention. One such incident was the Jeep Cherokee hack in 2015. Security researchers remotely exploited a vulnerability in the vehicle's entertainment system, demonstrating the potential for catastrophic consequences. This event underscored the urgency of addressing cybersecurity in the automotive industry.

Autonomous Vehicles and New Horizons

The push toward autonomous vehicles adds an extra layer of complexity to automotive cybersecurity. Self-driving cars rely on an intricate network of sensors, communication systems, and AI algorithms. Ensuring the security of these systems is paramount to prevent malicious interference and potential accidents.

As we approach the third decade of the 21st century, automotive cybersecurity has become a multidisciplinary field, involving software engineers, cryptographers, and ethical hackers working alongside traditional automotive engineers. It's a domain where innovation and vigilance are in constant tension, as manufacturers strive to develop cutting-edge features while protecting vehicles from cyber threats.

The Road Ahead

In the pursuit of innovation and safety, the automotive industry is on an ever-evolving journey in the realm of cybersecurity. It's a journey marked by historical developments, challenges, and a commitment to safeguarding the future of transportation.

In this book, we will delve deeper into the world of automotive cybersecurity, exploring the various components of modern vehicles, the threats and vulnerabilities they face, the regulations and standards that guide the industry, and the security measures and best practices needed to protect vehicles from cyberattacks. We will also examine real-world case studies, and gaze into the crystal ball to explore future trends in automotive cybersecurity.

The journey is just beginning, and our understanding of automotive cybersecurity is bound to evolve further. So, fasten your seatbelts as we embark on this journey through the digital age on wheels, where security and innovation collide in the fast lane.

The importance of cybersecurity in modern vehicles

As the sun rises on the 21st century, the automotive industry stands at a crossroads. Modern vehicles are no longer mere modes of transportation; they are sophisticated, interconnected machines that epitomize the fusion of digital technology and mobility. While this convergence has brought unparalleled convenience, comfort, and safety to our lives, it has also ushered in a new era of vulnerability - one where the integrity of our vehicles is under constant siege from cyber threats. In this age, automotive cybersecurity emerges as an indispensable shield, guarding against the perils of an increasingly digital and interconnected world.

The Automotive Metamorphosis

The journey from the first automobiles of the late 19th century to the modern, computerized vehicles of today is an astonishing tale of human ingenuity. Early cars were mechanical wonders, relying on engines and gears, with minimal electronics, to propel passengers from one point to another. They were, in essence, mechanical marvels with little digital presence.

The transformation that has taken place over the past few decades is nothing short of remarkable. Modern vehicles are far more than just means of conveyance; they are data-rich, computer-controlled systems on wheels. These technological leaps have translated into safer and more efficient transportation. Anti-lock braking systems, airbags, advanced driver assistance systems (ADAS), infotainment, and telematics systems have revolutionized the driving experience. Yet, each of these advances introduces a digital component into our vehicles.

Digital Intrusion: A New Threat Landscape

The very features that have made our vehicles safer, more efficient, and more enjoyable to drive have unwittingly given rise to an entirely new threat landscape. The increased digitization and connectivity in vehicles have opened up avenues for cyberattacks that were once inconceivable.

Imagine a scenario where an attacker can remotely access your car's control systems, disabling brakes, tampering with steering, or even taking control of the vehicle while you're driving. This is no longer a figment of the imagination; it's a sobering reality. As vehicles become more interconnected, they become increasingly vulnerable to a range of cyber threats, including hacking, data theft, and system manipulation.

The Internet of Things on Wheels

The concept of the Internet of Things (IoT) has permeated every facet of modern life. In vehicles, this is manifested in the emergence of the "Internet of Vehicles" (IoV). Cars are no longer standalone machines; they are nodes in a vast network, communicating with other vehicles, infrastructure, and even the cloud. This interconnectivity, while offering tremendous potential for improving traffic management, fuel efficiency, and safety, also exposes vehicles to cyber threats from various angles.

Modern cars contain multiple Electronic Control Units (ECUs) that control different aspects of vehicle operation. These ECUs are interconnected via communication networks, such as the Controller Area Network (CAN) or Ethernet. This interconnected web of components makes vehicles highly susceptible to cyberattacks. The threat could come from a compromised ECU, a manipulated data packet on the CAN bus, or a malicious software update.

The Stakes Are High

The importance of automotive cybersecurity cannot be overstated, as the stakes are incredibly high. A successful cyberattack on a vehicle can result in devastating consequences. These risks extend far beyond the individual driver or passengers and ripple out into society at large.

Consider, for instance, the implications of a cyberattack on a fleet of autonomous vehicles used for public transportation or delivery services. If attackers were to gain control of these vehicles, they could disrupt vital services, potentially leading to accidents, economic losses, and widespread chaos.

Moreover, modern vehicles collect an abundance of personal and sensitive data. They know where we've been, who we've communicated with, and even the condition of our health. This treasure trove of information is an attractive target for cybercriminals, who can exploit it for various malicious purposes, including identity theft and financial fraud.

In addition to data theft and physical control, the consequences of automotive cyberattacks could extend to privacy invasion, safety compromise, and even national security threats. The potential for wide-ranging disruption underscores the gravity of the situation.

Regulations and Standards

Recognizing the critical need for automotive cybersecurity, governments and industry organizations have stepped in to establish regulations and standards. These measures aim to ensure that manufacturers take the necessary steps to protect vehicles and the data they collect.

In the United States, the SPY Car Act was introduced to create federal regulations concerning vehicle cybersecurity. In Europe, the General Data Protection Regulation (GDPR) places specific requirements on vehicle manufacturers regarding data protection. Globally, organizations like the Society of Automotive Engineers (SAE) have developed standards such as ISO/SAE 21434, which provide guidance on vehicle cybersecurity.

These regulations and standards are essential in holding manufacturers accountable and driving the adoption of security practices across the automotive industry. They also serve to inform consumers, enabling them to make informed choices about the vehicles they drive.

Trust in the Age of Connectivity

Trust is the bedrock of the automotive industry. When we step into a car, we trust it to transport us safely to our destination. In the digital age, this trust extends to the technology underpinning our vehicles. We rely on these systems to work seamlessly and securely.

The importance of automotive cybersecurity lies in preserving and bolstering this trust. When consumers trust that their vehicles are secure from cyber threats, they can embrace the benefits of connectivity without fear. This trust encourages the adoption of innovative technologies and fuels the industry's growth.

Closing Thoughts

As we embark on this exploration of automotive cybersecurity, it is important to recognize that the digital age on wheels is both a boon and a challenge. The journey from purely mechanical vehicles to highly digitized machines has introduced new risks that demand our attention and expertise.

In this book, we will delve deeper into the various components of modern vehicles, the specific threats and vulnerabilities they face, and the security measures and best practices essential for safeguarding vehicles against cyberattacks. We will also examine real-world case studies to learn from past incidents and project into the future to understand the evolving landscape of automotive cybersecurity.

The path ahead is fraught with challenges and opportunities, and the importance of automotive cybersecurity cannot be overemphasized. By the time we conclude this exploration, you will be better equipped to navigate the digital age on wheels, knowing how to protect yourself and your vehicle in this brave new world of mobility.

Chapter 1: Components of Modern Vehicles

Electronic Control Units (ECUs)

In the realm of modern vehicles, Electronic Control Units (ECUs) stand as the silent orchestrators behind the scenes, governing nearly every aspect of the automobile's functionality. These unassuming hardware modules, resembling miniature computers, are the technological heart of the vehicle. ECUs are not just integral; they are mission-critical to ensure the efficient and safe operation of contemporary automobiles.

The ECU's Digital Command

An Electronic Control Unit (ECU) is a compact computing device designed to manage specific functions within a vehicle. It does so by processing and analyzing data from various sensors and, in response, issuing commands to corresponding actuators. In essence, ECUs serve as the interpreters between the analog world of a vehicle's mechanical and electrical systems and the digital world of computational logic.

As modern vehicles continue to evolve and embrace digital transformation, the number of ECUs within a single car has proliferated. Each ECU specializes in controlling a discrete set of functions, making it possible for today's cars to be multifaceted, efficient, and, most importantly, safe.

The Proliferation of ECUs

The digitization of automotive systems has heralded a profound transformation. In the early days of vehicular electronics, vehicles hosted a limited number of ECUs, typically managing the engine, transmission, and perhaps a few basic functions. Fast forward to the 21st century, and the automotive landscape has been irrevocably altered.

A modern automobile can house upwards of a hundred ECUs, each responsible for specific tasks. These tasks encompass engine management, transmission control, safety systems (such as airbags and anti-lock brakes), advanced driver assistance systems (ADAS), infotainment systems, climate control, and more. This proliferation of ECUs is the result of the increased complexity of vehicles, which now incorporate a diverse array of systems, including engine control, emissions control, body control, powertrain control, and more.

Functionality Across the Automotive Spectrum

ECUs in modern vehicles are categorized into various types, each tailored to a specific domain. The primary ECU categories include:

> Engine Control Unit (ECU): The Engine Control Unit serves as the brain of the vehicle's powerplant, regulating fuel injection, ignition timing, and various other parameters to optimize engine performance, fuel efficiency, and emissions.

> Transmission Control Unit (TCU): The Transmission Control Unit manages the operation of the transmission, ensuring smooth gear shifts and optimizing transmission performance.

> Body Control Module (BCM): The Body Control Module takes charge of functions related to the vehicle's body, including lighting, power windows, door locks, and security features like keyless entry systems.

Airbag Control Module (ACM): The Airbag Control Module is dedicated to the safety of passengers and deploys airbags when a collision is detected.

Antilock Braking System (ABS) Control Module: The ABS Control Module monitors wheel speed and applies or releases brake pressure to prevent wheel lockup during hard braking, enhancing vehicle stability and safety.

Infotainment Control Module (ICM): The Infotainment Control Module governs the vehicle's multimedia and entertainment features, including navigation, audio, and connectivity to external devices.

Climate Control Module (CCM): The Climate Control Module regulates heating, ventilation, and air conditioning (HVAC) systems to maintain the desired cabin temperature.

Advanced Driver Assistance Systems (ADAS) Control Modules: ADAS ECUs manage features like adaptive cruise control, lane-keeping assist, collision avoidance systems, and parking assistance.

Real-Time Data Processing

ECUs are designed to operate in real-time, continuously collecting data from various sensors. These sensors are strategically placed throughout the vehicle, monitoring parameters such as engine temperature, vehicle speed, tire pressure, steering angle, and much more. This data is relayed to the corresponding ECUs, which analyze it and make instantaneous decisions to adjust the vehicle's operation.

For instance, the Engine Control Unit (ECU) may receive input from an oxygen sensor in the exhaust system, indicating the air-fuel mixture is too rich. In response, the ECU adjusts the fuel injection to optimize combustion efficiency. This process occurs seamlessly and within milliseconds.

The continuous loop of data collection, processing, and response is what makes modern vehicles responsive, efficient, and safe. However, it also introduces vulnerabilities, as any interruption in this loop could lead to malfunctions or cyberattacks.

Interconnectedness and Communication

The modern vehicle is a complex network of interconnected ECUs, and communication between these units is facilitated through various protocols and networks. The Controller Area Network (CAN) is one of the most widely used communication standards in the automotive industry. It allows ECUs to exchange data in a standardized way, enabling seamless communication between disparate systems.

For example, the Engine Control Unit (ECU) may communicate with the Transmission Control Unit (TCU) to ensure that the engine's performance aligns with the transmission's gear shifts, optimizing power delivery and fuel efficiency.

Furthermore, emerging technologies such as Ethernet and FlexRay are playing increasingly pivotal roles in the high-speed data communication networks within vehicles, especially in modern, highly digitized cars.

Cybersecurity Implications

The growing number of ECUs and their interconnectedness raise significant cybersecurity concerns. Each ECU represents a potential entry point for malicious actors. If an attacker gains access to a single ECU, they may exploit it to infiltrate other systems, potentially taking control of critical vehicle functions.

Cybersecurity measures, such as secure boot processes, encryption, and intrusion detection systems, are essential to protect ECUs from unauthorized access and manipulation. Ensuring the security of these modules is paramount, not only to safeguard drivers and passengers but also to maintain public trust in the rapidly evolving digital automotive landscape.

Evolving Role in Autonomous Vehicles

As we hurtle toward an era of autonomous vehicles, the role of ECUs becomes even more crucial. Self-driving cars rely extensively on data processing and real-time decision-making, making the performance of ECUs integral to their safety and functionality.

ADAS ECUs, for instance, will become central to ensuring the safety and navigation of autonomous vehicles. These modules will handle complex tasks such as identifying obstacles, predicting road conditions, and making split-second decisions to avoid accidents.

The Road Ahead

In a world where the digital realm merges seamlessly with the physical, Electronic Control Units (ECUs) take center stage in modern vehicles. They are the unassuming commanders of the automotive orchestra, regulating everything from engine performance to infotainment systems, safety features to autonomous driving capabilities. In this book, we will delve deeper into the technical intricacies of ECUs, exploring their significance in modern vehicles, their functions, and the pivotal role they play in the automotive ecosystem. We will also scrutinize the cybersecurity challenges and advancements that are shaping the future of ECUs and the vehicles they command.

The road ahead is one of constant evolution, where ECUs will continue to evolve, adapt, and revolutionize the automotive landscape. As we embark on this technical exploration, we will navigate the complexities of the digital automotive age, understanding the mechanisms that underpin the vehicles we drive, and the future of the ever-evolving automotive

Communication networks (CAN, LIN, Ethernet)

In the contemporary automotive landscape, the proliferation of electronic systems and digital components has revolutionized the way vehicles function. At the heart of this digital transformation lie communication networks that enable seamless data exchange among various Electronic Control Units (ECUs) and sensors. In this technical exploration, we will delve into the intricate world of automotive communication networks, focusing on three key technologies: Controller Area Network (CAN), Local Interconnect Network (LIN), and Ethernet. These networks are the conduits through which vital data flows, and understanding their technical intricacies is essential for comprehending the modern automobile's digital complexity.

Controller Area Network (CAN)

The Backbone of Automotive Communication

Controller Area Network (CAN) is the linchpin of communication networks in modern vehicles. Developed by

Robert Bosch GmbH in the 1980s, CAN has since become the de facto standard for in-vehicle communication. It is renowned for its robustness, reliability, and real-time capabilities, making it the go-to choice for critical automotive systems.

Technical Aspects of CAN

Data Link Layer: CAN operates using a two-layer model, with the Data Link Layer responsible for managing message transmission. It employs a unique non-destructive bitwise arbitration mechanism that ensures smooth data transfer even in the presence of collisions.

Frame Structure: CAN messages are structured into frames, with two primary formats: Standard Frame Format (SFF) and Extended Frame Format (EFF). SFF uses 11-bit message identifiers, while EFF employs 29-bit identifiers, enabling a vast number of unique addresses for various ECUs.

Bit Rate: CAN allows for different bit rates, ranging from 125 kbit/s to 1 Mbit/s. The selection of bit rate depends on the specific application's requirements, with lower bit rates used for less time-critical applications and higher bit rates for faster data transfer.

Data Integrity: CAN includes built-in error-checking mechanisms, such as cyclic redundancy checks (CRCs) and checksums, to ensure data integrity during transmission.

Bus Topology: In most vehicles, CAN uses a two-wire bus topology, known as CAN High (CAN-H) and CAN Low (CAN-L). This differential signaling scheme is resilient to electromagnetic interference and provides high noise immunity.

Multi-Master: CAN operates on a multi-master principle, meaning that multiple ECUs can transmit and receive messages simultaneously. The arbitration process resolves conflicts and ensures data consistency.

Applications of CAN

CAN is the backbone of the automotive communication network, responsible for managing critical systems such as the Engine Control Unit (ECU), Transmission Control Unit (TCU), and Anti-lock Braking System (ABS). These systems require real-time, deterministic communication, and CAN's reliability makes it the ideal choice.

Local Interconnect Network (LIN)

Simplifying Communication for Non-Critical Systems

While CAN excels in managing critical systems, there are many non-critical applications within a vehicle that require a more cost-effective and simplified communication network. This is where the Local Interconnect Network (LIN) steps in. LIN is a complementary protocol to CAN, specifically designed for tasks that don't require the real-time precision of CAN.

Technical Aspects of LIN

Master-Slave Topology: LIN employs a master-slave topology, where one ECU acts as the master and controls multiple slave nodes. The master initiates communication, while slaves respond to requests.

Message Framing: LIN messages are structured into frames, including header and response parts. Frames are relatively simple and consist of a few bytes of data, making them ideal for low-complexity applications.

Low Bit Rate: LIN typically operates at lower bit rates, usually around 19.2 kbit/s. This slower speed is adequate for tasks like controlling window switches, door locks, and interior lighting.

Message Scheduling: LIN messages are scheduled, and the master node dictates the timing and frequency of messages. This deterministic scheduling simplifies network management.

Low Power: LIN is known for its low power consumption, making it suitable for applications where energy efficiency is essential.

Applications of LIN

LIN is commonly found in non-essential vehicle systems, such as power windows, seat adjustment, and interior lighting. Its simplified architecture and low cost make it a practical choice for applications that don't require the real-time response of CAN.

Ethernet in Automotive

Cat-6 Cables on Wheels: The Evolution of Automotive Networking

The integration of advanced driver assistance systems (ADAS), infotainment, and autonomous features necessitates a high-speed, high-bandwidth network. Ethernet, with its high data transfer capabilities, is gaining traction in the automotive industry to meet these demands.

Technical Aspects of Ethernet

High Data Rate: Ethernet in vehicles typically operates at 100 Mbps or 1 Gbps. This high bandwidth is crucial for supporting bandwidth-intensive applications like high-definition video streaming and sensor data.

IP-based Protocol: Ethernet uses the Internet Protocol (IP) for communication, making it highly compatible with existing IT infrastructure and allowing for easier integration of vehicle networks with external networks, such as the internet.

Switched Architecture: Unlike CAN or LIN, Ethernet often employs a switched architecture, which is more akin to a traditional computer network. This allows for more efficient data transmission and reduces network congestion.

Broad ECU Integration: Ethernet is well-suited for a wide range of ECUs, including those that require high bandwidth, such as cameras, radar systems, and infotainment units.

Deterministic Ethernet: In addition to standard Ethernet, there are efforts to bring deterministic characteristics to Ethernet for use in safety-critical applications. Protocols like Time-Sensitive Networking (TSN) aim to provide real-time capabilities to Ethernet.

Applications of Ethernet

Ethernet is primarily employed in advanced systems like ADAS, infotainment, and autonomous driving. It is critical for high-resolution camera systems, radar processing, and sensor fusion. As vehicles become more like data centers on wheels, Ethernet's high-speed data transfer capabilities are indispensable.

Integration Challenges and Opportunities

While these communication networks serve distinct purposes, modern vehicles often integrate all three—CAN,

LIN, and Ethernet—to create a comprehensive network architecture. The challenge lies in harmonizing these technologies to facilitate the seamless exchange of data among diverse ECUs.

Integration is further complicated by the need for cybersecurity. As vehicles become more interconnected, the attack surface for cyber threats expands. Safeguarding these communication networks against intrusions is an ongoing priority in the automotive industry.

Conclusion

The world of automotive communication networks is one of intricate design, real-time precision, and evolving standards. CAN, LIN, and Ethernet, each with its unique characteristics, play critical roles in enabling the digital orchestration of modern vehicles. As technology continues to advance and vehicles become more autonomous and connected, these networks will remain central to the efficient, safe, and data-rich operation of our automobiles. Understanding their technical intricacies is paramount to grasping the evolving complexity of the digital automotive landscape and the technical challenges that lie ahead.

Sensors and Actuators in Modern Vehicles:

Modern vehicles are teeming with sensors and actuators, the eyes and hands of the automotive world. These components, often hidden from view, are the unsung heroes that enable your car to perceive its surroundings, make critical decisions, and execute precise actions. In this technical exploration, we will delve into the intricate world of sensors and actuators, understanding their diverse types, functions, and the pivotal roles they play in the operation of contemporary automobiles.

Sensors in Modern Vehicles

Sensing the World

Sensors are the sensory organs of a vehicle, responsible for detecting and measuring various physical and environmental parameters. They convert real-world phenomena, such as temperature, pressure, or light, into electrical signals that can be interpreted by Electronic Control Units (ECUs) to make informed decisions. The wide array of sensors found in modern vehicles can be categorized based on their function and application.

1. Temperature Sensors:

- Engine Coolant Temperature Sensor: This sensor monitors the temperature of the engine coolant. It ensures that the engine operates within the optimal temperature range by providing data to the Engine Control Unit (ECU) for adjustments to the fuel-air mixture.
- Ambient Air Temperature Sensor: Located in the exterior of the vehicle, this sensor measures the temperature of the air, which is used for climate control systems and to display external temperature readings to the driver.

2. Pressure Sensors:

- Manifold Absolute Pressure (MAP) Sensor: The MAP sensor measures the pressure of air in the intake manifold, helping the ECU optimize air-fuel mixture for engine performance and emissions control.
- Tire Pressure Monitoring System (TPMS) Sensor: TPMS sensors are mounted in each tire to monitor

tire pressure and alert the driver if pressure drops below a safe threshold.

3. Position Sensors:
   - Throttle Position Sensor (TPS): The TPS provides data on the position of the throttle plate. This information is used by the ECU to control engine performance and fuel delivery.
   - Crankshaft Position Sensor: This sensor determines the rotational position of the crankshaft, enabling precise ignition timing and fuel injection control.

4. Light and Optical Sensors:
   - Light Sensors (Photocells): These sensors detect ambient light levels, allowing automatic adjustment of the vehicle's lighting systems, such as automatic headlamp control.
   - Rain Sensors: Rain sensors use optical technology to detect the presence of raindrops on the windshield, activating automatic wipers.

5. Inertial Sensors:
   - Accelerometers and Gyroscopes: These sensors measure acceleration and angular velocity, providing data to stability control and advanced driver assistance systems (ADAS) like electronic stability control and roll-over protection.

6. Proximity Sensors:
   - Ultrasonic Parking Sensors: Used in parking assistance systems, ultrasonic sensors emit sound waves to detect obstacles around the vehicle and provide proximity warnings.
   - Radar Sensors: Radar sensors are crucial for adaptive cruise control and collision avoidance

systems, using radar waves to detect objects in the vehicle's path.

7. Gas Sensors:

- Oxygen Sensors (O2 Sensors): O2 sensors measure the oxygen content in the exhaust gases. The ECU uses this data to fine-tune the air-fuel mixture for optimal combustion and emissions control.
- Carbon Dioxide (CO_2) Sensors: Some modern vehicles include CO_2 sensors as part of their climate control systems to monitor air quality inside the cabin.

Actuators in Modern Vehicles

Executing Decisions with Precision

Actuators are the dynamic executors in a vehicle, responding to commands from ECUs and carrying out precise actions. They translate electrical signals into mechanical movements, making it possible for the vehicle to accelerate, brake, steer, and perform other critical functions.

1. Fuel Injectors:

Fuel injectors are responsible for delivering precise amounts of fuel into the engine's cylinders. The ECU controls their operation, determining the duration and timing of each injection.

2. Spark Plugs:

Spark plugs initiate the combustion process by generating an electrical spark. They are controlled by the ECU and are timed to ignite the air-fuel mixture in the engine.

3. Solenoids:

Solenoids are versatile actuators used in various vehicle systems:

- Starter Solenoid: The starter solenoid engages the starter motor to crank the engine when the key is turned.
- Transmission Solenoids: These actuate gear changes in automatic transmissions based on signals from the Transmission Control Unit (TCU).
- Turbocharger Wastegate Solenoid: This solenoid controls the wastegate, regulating boost pressure in turbocharged engines.

4. Throttle Actuators:

In electronic throttle control systems, a throttle actuator modulates the position of the throttle plate. It ensures precise control of engine power based on driver input and ECU commands.

5. Brake Actuators:
- Brake Calipers: In anti-lock braking systems (ABS), brake calipers can apply and release the brakes rapidly to prevent wheel lockup.
- Brake Booster: The brake booster multiplies the force applied to the brake pedal, making braking more efficient. It is controlled by the brake pedal position sensor.

6. Steering Actuators:
- Electric Power Steering (EPS) Motors: In EPS systems, electric motors assist in steering by applying torque to the steering column based on driver input and vehicle speed.

7. Transmission Actuators:
- Shift Solenoids: These actuators are used in automatic transmissions to control gear changes. The TCU commands them to engage and disengage clutches and bands.

8. HVAC Actuators:
- Blend Door Actuators: These actuators control the position of blend doors in the HVAC system, regulating the mix of hot and cold air to maintain cabin temperature.
- Recirculation Door Actuators: They control the recirculation of air within the cabin, managing air quality and efficiency.

9. Door Lock Actuators:

Door lock actuators are responsible for locking and unlocking the vehicle's doors based on input from the key fob or interior switches.

Challenges and Advancements in Sensors and Actuators

As vehicles become more sophisticated and embrace automation and electrification, sensors and actuators face new challenges and opportunities:
- Integration of Sensor Data: Advanced driver assistance systems (ADAS) and autonomous driving require the seamless integration of data from multiple sensors, including radar, lidar, cameras, and more.
- Electric and Autonomous Vehicles: Electric vehicles (EVs) and autonomous vehicles depend heavily on sensors and actuators for precise control and safety. LiDAR sensors, in particular, are crucial for mapping the surroundings of autonomous vehicles.
- Redundancy and Safety: Ensuring the safety and reliability of sensor and actuator systems is paramount. Redundancy and fail-safes are essential in critical applications like braking and steering.
- Miniaturization and Durability: Sensors and actuators are becoming smaller and more durable,

with advancements in materials and manufacturing techniques. They must withstand harsh environmental conditions and temperature variations.

Conclusion

Sensors and actuators are the technical backbone of modern vehicles, enabling precise control, safety, and efficiency. As the automotive industry continues to evolve, the role of these components becomes increasingly pivotal. They are not just instruments and executors; they are the conduits through which vehicles perceive, interpret, and interact with the world around them. Understanding their technical intricacies is essential for grasping the complexity of modern automobiles and the technical challenges and advancements that lie ahead in the ever-evolving automotive ecosystem.

Chapter 2: Threats and Vulnerabilities

Hacking and Exploitation

The increasing digitization and connectivity of modern vehicles have introduced a new realm of cybersecurity challenges. Automotive cybersecurity is a critical field, as the potential consequences of a successful attack can be severe, ranging from privacy breaches to vehicle control. In this technical exploration, we will delve into various hacking and exploitation examples in the automotive context, shedding light on the vulnerabilities that exist and the potential threats that lurk within the digital fortresses on wheels.

1. Remote Keyless Entry (RKE) Exploitation

Vulnerability: Many modern vehicles employ keyless entry systems, allowing drivers to unlock and start their vehicles with key fobs that communicate with the car using radio frequency (RF) signals.

Exploitation: Attackers can intercept and replicate the RF signals transmitted by the key fob, enabling them to unlock and start the vehicle without physical access to the key. This is often achieved through signal relay attacks, where one attacker stands near the key fob, while another stands near the vehicle. The first attacker captures the key fob's signal and relays it to the second attacker, who uses it to unlock and start the vehicle.

2. Diagnostic Port Exploitation

Vulnerability: The On-Board Diagnostics II (OBD-II) port is a standard feature in most vehicles, designed for vehicle diagnostics and maintenance. It provides access to various vehicle systems.

Exploitation: Malicious actors can exploit the OBD-II port to gain access to the vehicle's internal network, compromising systems like the Engine Control Unit (ECU). This allows them to manipulate engine performance, disable safety features, or even inject malware into the vehicle's software. Attacks on the OBD-II port often require physical access, but the potential consequences can be severe.

3. Wireless Tire Pressure Monitoring System (TPMS) Attacks

Vulnerability: TPMS sensors are equipped with wireless communication capabilities to transmit tire pressure data to the vehicle's ECU. These sensors are often unprotected.

Exploitation: Attackers can compromise the TPMS system by sending malicious signals, causing false tire pressure readings. This can lead to inaccurate alerts, causing drivers to ignore real safety warnings. In some cases, attackers can even use TPMS as an entry point to infiltrate the vehicle's internal network.

4. Infotainment System Vulnerabilities

Vulnerability: Modern vehicles are equipped with advanced infotainment systems that connect to external networks, such as the internet, to provide entertainment and navigation services.

Exploitation: Cybercriminals can exploit vulnerabilities in infotainment systems to gain access to the vehicle's internal network. They may do this through malicious software updates or by injecting malware into the infotainment system. Once inside the vehicle's network, attackers can potentially take control of critical systems, including the engine and brakes.

5. Malicious Firmware Updates

Vulnerability: Vehicles often receive firmware and software updates to improve performance, security, and add new features. However, the process of updating firmware can be vulnerable to attack.

Exploitation: Attackers can compromise the update process by intercepting and modifying the firmware updates sent to the vehicle. This can result in the installation of malicious firmware, which can grant unauthorized access and control over various vehicle systems.

6. Autonomous Vehicle Spoofing

Vulnerability: Autonomous vehicles rely on a combination of sensors, including lidar, radar, and cameras, to navigate and make real-time decisions. These sensors can be vulnerable to spoofing.

Exploitation: Attackers can use jamming or spoofing techniques to disrupt the operation of autonomous vehicles. By sending false sensor data or interfering with sensor signals, attackers can confuse the vehicle's perception system and potentially cause it to make incorrect decisions.

7. Remote Telematics Exploitation

Vulnerability: Many vehicles are equipped with telematics systems that allow remote monitoring and control of the vehicle. These systems are often accessible via mobile apps or web portals.

Exploitation: If telematics systems are not adequately secured, attackers can gain unauthorized access to the vehicle's functions. They may be able to locate and unlock the vehicle, start the engine, and access sensitive information. In some cases, attackers have even disabled vehicles remotely.

8. Over-the-Air (OTA) Update Vulnerabilities

Vulnerability: Many vehicles support OTA updates, allowing manufacturers to deliver software updates and patches remotely.

Exploitation: Attackers can potentially intercept and manipulate OTA updates, injecting malicious code into the vehicle's software. This can compromise the vehicle's security and provide a foothold for further attacks.

9. ECU Firmware Attacks

Vulnerability: Electronic Control Units (ECUs) control critical vehicle functions and are susceptible to attacks if their firmware is not adequately protected.

Exploitation: Attackers can target ECU firmware, either by exploiting vulnerabilities in the firmware itself or by attacking the ECU's communication interfaces. Once compromised, they can manipulate engine performance, brakes, and other safety-critical systems.

10. Vulnerabilities in In-Vehicle Networks

Vulnerability: Modern vehicles often feature multiple in-vehicle networks, including the Controller Area Network (CAN), which can be vulnerable to intrusion.

Exploitation: Attackers may gain access to in-vehicle networks through vulnerabilities in the network architecture or by exploiting unsecured access points. Once inside, they can propagate through the network, potentially taking control of multiple ECUs.

Mitigation and Defense

To defend against these potential threats and vulnerabilities, the automotive industry has made significant advancements in cybersecurity. These measures include:

- Intrusion Detection Systems (IDS): IDS can detect unauthorized access or malicious activity within the vehicle's network and trigger alerts or countermeasures.

- Secure Boot Processes: Implementing secure boot processes for ECUs ensures that only trusted and authenticated firmware is loaded.
- Encryption and Authentication: Encrypting communication channels and requiring authentication for software updates and access to critical vehicle systems.
- Firewalls: Deploying firewalls within the vehicle's network to monitor and control incoming and outgoing traffic.
- Collaborative Efforts: Industry standards like ISO/SAE 21434 and regulations like the SPY Car Act encourage automakers to implement robust cybersecurity measures.

Conclusion

As vehicles become increasingly digital and interconnected, the potential for hacking and exploitation grows. While these examples illustrate vulnerabilities in automotive cybersecurity, it is essential to recognize that the industry is actively working to address these issues. Continuous research, vigilant cybersecurity practices, and collaborative efforts are fundamental to securing the digital fortresses on wheels and ensuring the safety and integrity of modern vehicles.

The Potential Consequences of Cyber Attacks

The integration of digital technology into modern vehicles has opened up new avenues for convenience, connectivity, and automation. However, it has also exposed vehicles to a range of cyber threats that can have significant and sometimes life-threatening consequences. In this exploration, we will discuss the potential consequences of cyberattacks in automotive cybersecurity, spanning technical, safety, and privacy aspects.

1. Safety Compromises

One of the most critical concerns in automotive cybersecurity is the potential compromise of safety systems. Modern vehicles rely heavily on electronic control units (ECUs) to manage safety-critical functions, such as anti-lock braking systems (ABS), electronic stability control (ESC), airbag deployment, and even autonomous driving features. Cyberattacks that target these systems can result in:

- Loss of Control: Attackers can take control of vehicle systems, potentially overriding steering, braking, and acceleration functions. This can lead to a loss of control and pose a severe safety risk.
- Sudden Braking or Acceleration: Malicious actors could engage the brakes or accelerator without driver input, leading to accidents, especially in high-speed situations.
- Airbag Deployment: Unauthorized airbag deployment, or the disabling of airbags, can put occupants at risk during a collision.
- Autonomous Vehicle Manipulation: Autonomous vehicles are vulnerable to attacks that can manipulate sensor data or control systems, causing accidents or misguiding the vehicle.

2. Physical Harm and Fatalities

In the worst-case scenario, cyberattacks on vehicles can result in physical harm and even fatalities. The potential consequences include:

- Accidents: Manipulating vehicle systems can lead to accidents, injuries, and fatalities, especially in situations where drivers have limited time to react to unexpected actions.
- Rollovers and Collisions: Steering and braking system attacks could cause rollovers and collisions, particularly in high-speed scenarios.
- Pedestrian and Cyclist Risks: A compromised vehicle may pose risks to pedestrians and cyclists, especially in urban settings.

3. Privacy Violations

Modern vehicles gather extensive data about drivers and passengers, including locations, driving habits, and even personal information synced from smartphones. Cyberattacks can result in severe privacy violations, such as:

- Location Tracking: Attackers may access and misuse location data, potentially leading to stalking or targeted theft.
- Personal Information Theft: In-vehicle infotainment systems and smartphones connected to the vehicle could expose personal data if compromised. This could lead to identity theft or fraud.
- Voice and Video Surveillance: Some vehicles feature voice-activated systems and in-cabin cameras, which, if hacked, can be used for eavesdropping or spying on occupants.

4. Financial Consequences

Cyberattacks on vehicles can have financial repercussions for both vehicle owners and automakers:

- Repair Costs: After a successful cyberattack, the vehicle may require extensive repairs to restore functionality, incurring significant costs for vehicle owners.
- Recalls and Liability: Automakers may be forced to issue recalls if vulnerabilities are discovered, resulting in substantial financial implications. Liability claims may also arise if accidents occur due to cyberattacks.
- Insurance Premiums: Insurers may increase premiums for vehicles that have been victims of cyberattacks, affecting vehicle owners' finances.

5. Brand Damage

A significant cyberattack on an automaker's vehicles can severely damage its reputation and brand image:

- Loss of Trust: Customers may lose trust in the brand's commitment to safety and security, leading to a decline in sales and market value.
- Litigation: Legal action and class-action lawsuits may be brought against automakers, further harming their image and finances.

6. Vehicle Theft and Resale Value Reduction

Cyberattacks can lead to vehicle theft and a reduction in the resale value of compromised vehicles:

- Key Fob Manipulation: Some attacks target keyless entry and ignition systems, enabling the theft of vehicles.
- Reduced Resale Value: Vehicles with a history of cyberattacks may experience a drop in resale value, affecting owners' finances.

7. Supply Chain Risks

Automakers rely on complex supply chains involving numerous vendors and suppliers. Cyberattacks can have a cascading effect:

- Supply Chain Disruptions: Attacks on suppliers may disrupt the manufacturing and delivery of components, impacting automakers' production schedules.
- Contaminated Software and Components: Cyberattacks can introduce tainted software or components into vehicles, posing significant safety and security risks.

8. Regulatory and Legal Repercussions

The automotive industry is subject to various regulations and standards to ensure safety and security. Cyberattacks can result in:

- Regulatory Scrutiny: Cyberattacks may trigger regulatory investigations and the development of new cybersecurity standards for the industry.
- Legal Actions: Automakers could face legal actions and penalties for not adequately protecting their vehicles against cyber threats.

9. Psychological and Emotional Consequences

Drivers and passengers who experience a cyberattack on their vehicle may suffer from psychological and emotional consequences:

- Trauma: Being in a vehicle that experiences a cyberattack can be a traumatic experience, resulting in anxiety and emotional distress.
- Loss of Confidence: Drivers may lose confidence in the safety and reliability of their vehicles, affecting their overall well-being.

10. Vehicle-Infrastructure Attacks

In addition to vehicle-centric attacks, cyber threats can extend to the infrastructure, including traffic control systems and smart intersections. Consequences may include:

- Traffic Disruptions: Attacks on traffic control systems can disrupt traffic flow, leading to congestion, delays, and accidents.
- Emergency Response Challenges: Emergency services may be impeded in their ability to respond to incidents if communication systems are compromised.

11. Reputational Damage for the Automotive Industry

Beyond individual automakers, the automotive industry as a whole can face reputational damage:

- Consumer Perceptions: A high-profile cyberattack on one automaker can affect how consumers perceive the entire industry, leading to mistrust.
- Global Ramifications: Cyberattacks on vehicles are not confined to a single region. They can have global ramifications, affecting the industry on a worldwide scale.

12. Broader Implications for Autonomous Vehicles

As autonomous vehicles become more prevalent, the consequences of cyberattacks become even more significant:

- Massive Data Exposure: Autonomous vehicles generate vast amounts of data, and cyberattacks can expose this data, including sensitive mapping information.
- Traffic Disruptions: Attacks on autonomous vehicles can lead to traffic disruptions and significant safety

concerns, as these vehicles interact with human-driven vehicles.

- Impact on Urban Planning: Cyberattacks on autonomous vehicles could disrupt urban planning efforts, as cities invest in smart transportation systems that rely on autonomous vehicles for efficient traffic management.

13. International Relations and Cybersecurity Diplomacy

Cyberattacks on vehicles can have international implications:

- Cybersecurity Diplomacy: Governments and international organizations may need to engage in diplomacy and cooperation to address cross-border cyber threats to vehicles.
- Geopolitical Tensions: Cyberattacks on vehicles can exacerbate geopolitical tensions, especially if nation-states are involved.

Conclusion

The potential consequences of cyberattacks in automotive cybersecurity are multifaceted and extend beyond the technical realm to affect safety, privacy, finances, and the broader industry. As vehicles become more digitally connected and autonomous, the need for robust cybersecurity measures becomes increasingly critical. To mitigate these consequences, automakers, governments, and the cybersecurity community must work together to strengthen the resilience of vehicles and ensure the safety and security of those on the road.

Chapter 3: Regulations and Standards

Global Automotive Cybersecurity Standards

The proliferation of digital technology in modern vehicles has introduced new challenges related to cybersecurity. The increasing connectivity and complexity of automotive systems have made vehicles potential targets for cyber threats. To address these challenges, the automotive industry has adopted a set of global cybersecurity standards and guidelines aimed at safeguarding vehicles and their occupants from malicious attacks. In this technical discussion, we will delve into the key global automotive cybersecurity standards, exploring their technical details and significance in the ever-evolving landscape of automotive security.

ISO/SAE 21434: The Cornerstone of Automotive Cybersecurity

ISO/SAE 21434 is the foundational standard for automotive cybersecurity, developed collaboratively by the International Organization for Standardization (ISO) and the Society of Automotive Engineers (SAE). It outlines a comprehensive framework for establishing a cybersecurity management process for vehicles, covering the entire vehicle lifecycle from development and production to operation and decommissioning.

Key Components of ISO/SAE 21434:

> Security-by-Design Principles: The standard promotes the integration of cybersecurity throughout the vehicle's development process. It requires manufacturers to adopt a security-by-design

approach, identifying and addressing security risks at each stage.

Risk Assessment and Management: ISO/SAE 21434 mandates a thorough risk assessment process, identifying potential vulnerabilities, threats, and security requirements. This assessment helps in defining security objectives and selecting appropriate security measures.

Security Requirements: The standard emphasizes the establishment of security requirements tailored to the vehicle's architecture and functionality. These requirements encompass technical specifications and controls to mitigate identified risks.

Security Validation and Verification: ISO/SAE 21434 enforces rigorous testing and validation procedures. Manufacturers must verify that their security measures effectively mitigate identified risks. Testing includes vulnerability assessments and penetration testing.

Incident Response and Recovery: The standard outlines procedures for managing and responding to cybersecurity incidents. It requires manufacturers to establish an incident response plan, which includes identification, containment, eradication, and recovery steps.

Updates and Maintenance: ISO/SAE 21434 addresses the need for continuous monitoring and maintenance of cybersecurity measures. Manufacturers must update security measures to adapt to evolving threats and vulnerabilities.

Technical Implications of ISO/SAE 21434:

ISO/SAE 21434 has several technical implications for the automotive industry:

- Security Development Lifecycle (SDL): Manufacturers need to implement an SDL, which integrates security considerations into the software and hardware development process. This involves security reviews, threat modeling, and security testing at different development stages.
- Secure Boot Processes: ISO/SAE 21434 emphasizes the need for secure boot processes, ensuring that only authenticated and trusted software components are loaded during the vehicle's startup.
- Cryptographic Controls: The standard highlights the importance of cryptographic controls, including encryption for data in transit and at rest, digital signatures for software integrity, and secure key management.
- Communication Security: Vehicle networks and communication protocols must be secured to prevent eavesdropping, data manipulation, and unauthorized access. ISO/SAE 21434 requires the use of secure communication protocols.

UNECE WP.29 and its Cybersecurity Regulations

The United Nations Economic Commission for Europe (UNECE) WP.29 working group is responsible for shaping global automotive regulations. In 2021, WP.29 introduced a series of regulations that specifically address cybersecurity in vehicles, known as "UN Regulation No. 155 - Cybersecurity and Cybersecurity Management System."

Key Components of UN Regulation No. 155:

Cybersecurity Management System (CSMS): This regulation mandates the implementation of a CSMS by automotive manufacturers and suppliers. The CSMS outlines the processes and procedures for managing cybersecurity throughout the vehicle's lifecycle.

Security by Design: UN Regulation No. 155 requires manufacturers to incorporate security into the design and development of their vehicles. This encompasses risk assessment, security requirements, and validation and testing.

Cybersecurity Auditing: Independent auditors play a critical role in verifying that manufacturers adhere to cybersecurity standards and regulations. This auditing process assesses the manufacturer's CSMS to ensure its effectiveness.

Event Reporting: Manufacturers must establish processes for reporting and managing cybersecurity incidents. Timely reporting is crucial to address potential threats and vulnerabilities.

Technical Implications of UN Regulation No. 155:

UN Regulation No. 155 has several technical implications for the automotive industry:

- Threat Modeling and Risk Assessment: Manufacturers are required to conduct thorough threat modeling and risk assessments to identify potential vulnerabilities and threats within their vehicles.
- Continuous Monitoring: The regulation emphasizes the need for continuous monitoring of in-vehicle networks and systems. Anomalies should trigger

alerts and responses to address potential cyber threats.

- Remote Software Updates: Secure over-the-air (OTA) software updates are encouraged as a means to patch vulnerabilities and enhance vehicle security. Manufacturers must ensure the integrity and authenticity of OTA updates.
- Incident Response Plans: Manufacturers must have well-defined incident response plans in place, specifying how to detect, respond to, and recover from cybersecurity incidents.

Global Technical Regulations (GTRs) from WP.29

In addition to UN Regulation No. 155, the UNECE WP.29 working group has introduced other cybersecurity-related GTRs that provide technical standards and requirements for vehicle cybersecurity. These include:

GTR No. 1 (Cybersecurity): This GTR sets out the definitions and frameworks for vehicle cybersecurity and provides guidelines for cybersecurity management systems.

GTR No. 2 (Cybersecurity and Software Updates): GTR No. 2 addresses software updates and their impact on vehicle cybersecurity. It defines technical requirements for secure software updates and validation processes.

GTR No. 7 (Electronic Vehicle Controls and Displays): While not specific to cybersecurity, GTR No. 7 includes provisions related to the protection of electronically controlled systems from cyber threats.

China's GB/T 38570-2020: Automotive Cybersecurity Standards

China introduced GB/T 38570-2020, a set of national standards for automotive cybersecurity. These standards share commonalities with ISO/SAE 21434 but also have unique technical requirements. Key aspects of GB/T 38570-2020 include:

- Security Design Principles: Similar to ISO/SAE 21434, GB/T 38570-2020 promotes security-by-design principles, emphasizing the incorporation of security measures throughout the development process.
- Risk Assessment and Management: The standard requires risk assessments to identify potential vulnerabilities and threats, with an emphasis on cybersecurity impact analysis.
- Security Verification and Validation: Manufacturers must undertake security verification and validation activities to ensure that security measures are effective. This includes conducting penetration testing, code reviews, and security testing.
- Software and Firmware Integrity: GB/T 38570-2020 addresses software and firmware integrity, including measures to ensure that only trusted and authenticated software is used in the vehicle.
- Incident Response: Manufacturers must establish incident response procedures to address cybersecurity incidents promptly.

NIST Special Publication 800-183: Cybersecurity Practice Guide for IoT-Connected Vehicle

The National Institute of Standards and Technology (NIST) in the United States has developed Special Publication 800-183, which provides guidance on securing IoT-connected vehicles. While not a binding standard, it offers valuable technical insights and practices for enhancing vehicle cybersecurity.

Key elements of NIST Special Publication 800-183 include:

- Access Control: The guide recommends implementing strong access controls to restrict unauthorized access to vehicle systems and data.
- Data Protection: It emphasizes the need for data encryption, secure data transmission, and protection against unauthorized data access.
- Device Identity and Authentication: Manufacturers are advised to establish strong device identity and authentication mechanisms to ensure only authorized devices can interact with the vehicle.
- Security Monitoring and Incident Detection: The guide promotes continuous security monitoring and the use of intrusion detection systems to identify and respond to security incidents.
- Secure Software Development: NIST recommends secure software development practices, including code review and the use of software security testing tools.

Conclusion

Global automotive cybersecurity standards are critical in ensuring the safety and security of modern vehicles. ISO/SAE 21434, UN Regulation No. 155, and other related standards and regulations provide a technical foundation for manufacturers to integrate cybersecurity measures into their vehicles' design, development, and operation. These standards emphasize a security-by-design approach, risk assessment, incident response, and continuous monitoring, reflecting the evolving landscape of automotive cybersecurity. By adhering to these standards, the automotive industry can build trust with consumers and ensure that vehicles remain protected from cyber threats throughout their lifecycles.

Regional Regulations and Compliance

The automotive industry operates on a global scale, with vehicles crossing international borders regularly. This interconnectedness has led to the development of regional regulations and compliance frameworks that automakers must navigate to ensure their vehicles meet the required cybersecurity standards. In this technical exploration, we will delve into the key regional regulations and compliance requirements for automotive cybersecurity, covering the technical details and implications of these standards.

1. North America: The Role of the U.S. NHTSA and SAE J3061

U.S. National Highway Traffic Safety Administration (NHTSA):

The United States, through the National Highway Traffic Safety Administration (NHTSA), plays a significant role in setting automotive cybersecurity standards. While not a binding regulation, the NHTSA has published guidelines and best practices for vehicle cybersecurity.

- NHTSA's Technical Guidelines: These guidelines focus on the identification and mitigation of cybersecurity risks in vehicles. They recommend a security-by-design approach, vulnerability assessments, and risk management.

SAE J3061: Cybersecurity Guidebook for Cyber-Physical Vehicle Systems:

The Society of Automotive Engineers (SAE) has developed J3061, a guidebook that outlines best practices and technical guidelines for developing secure vehicle systems. It provides a comprehensive framework for automotive cybersecurity:

- Security by Design: SAE J3061 emphasizes integrating cybersecurity considerations into the vehicle development process, identifying potential threats and vulnerabilities.
- Risk Assessment and Management: The guidebook covers risk assessment methodologies to identify and prioritize cybersecurity risks.
- Security Validation and Verification: It outlines procedures for security testing and validation to ensure that cybersecurity measures effectively mitigate identified risks.
- Incident Response and Recovery: The guidebook provides guidance on managing and responding to cybersecurity incidents, including procedures for containment and recovery.

2. Europe: UNECE WP.29 and the EU's General Data Protection Regulation (GDPR)

UNECE WP.29 and UN Regulation No. 155:

The United Nations Economic Commission for Europe (UNECE) WP.29 working group is responsible for shaping global automotive regulations. In 2021, WP.29 introduced "UN Regulation No. 155 - Cybersecurity and Cybersecurity Management System," which sets out regulations and guidelines for vehicle cybersecurity. It emphasizes the need for a Cybersecurity Management System (CSMS) and independent auditing.

- Security by Design: UN Regulation No. 155 underscores the integration of security by design in vehicle development, similar to the principles in SAE J3061.
- Cybersecurity Auditing: The regulation introduces the role of independent auditors to verify compliance with cybersecurity standards. Auditors assess the effectiveness of the manufacturer's CSMS.

EU General Data Protection Regulation (GDPR):

While GDPR is primarily a data protection regulation, it has implications for vehicle cybersecurity, especially concerning data security and privacy. GDPR affects vehicle manufacturers and suppliers operating within the European Union and those processing the data of EU residents.

- Data Protection: GDPR requires the protection of personal data, and this extends to data collected and processed within vehicles. Manufacturers must implement technical and organizational measures to safeguard data against breaches.

3. China: GB/T 38570-2020 and the China Compulsory Certification (CCC)

GB/T 38570-2020: Automotive Cybersecurity Standards in China:

China introduced GB/T 38570-2020, a set of national standards for automotive cybersecurity. These standards share commonalities with ISO/SAE 21434 but also have unique technical requirements.

- Security Design Principles: GB/T 38570-2020 promotes security by design, emphasizing the need for manufacturers to consider cybersecurity from the vehicle's development phase.

- Risk Assessment and Management: The standards require risk assessments to identify potential vulnerabilities and threats, with a focus on cybersecurity impact analysis.
- Security Validation and Verification: Manufacturers must conduct security verification and validation activities to ensure the effectiveness of security measures. This includes penetration testing and security testing.
- Incident Response: GB/T 38570-2020 mandates manufacturers to establish procedures for responding to cybersecurity incidents.

China Compulsory Certification (CCC):

The China Compulsory Certification (CCC) is a mandatory certification system for a wide range of products, including automotive components. While CCC does not specifically focus on cybersecurity, it ensures that vehicles and their components meet certain safety and quality standards.

- Component Safety and Quality: Under CCC, components installed in vehicles, including electronic and electrical components, must meet safety and quality standards. These standards indirectly contribute to vehicle cybersecurity.

4. Japan: The Role of the Ministry of Land, Infrastructure, Transport, and Tourism (MLIT)

The Ministry of Land, Infrastructure, Transport, and Tourism (MLIT) in Japan oversees automotive regulations and standards. While Japan does not have specific automotive cybersecurity regulations, the government plays a role in shaping vehicle safety standards, which indirectly impact cybersecurity.

- Safety Standards: MLIT sets safety standards for vehicles, including electronic and electrical components. These standards indirectly contribute to ensuring the cybersecurity of vehicles sold in Japan.

5. South Korea: KNCSC (Korea National Computerization Security Center) Regulations

South Korea, through KNCSC, has introduced regulations aimed at enhancing the cybersecurity of connected vehicles. KNCSC regulations require automakers and suppliers to implement cybersecurity measures.

- Technical Guidelines: KNCSC regulations include technical guidelines for securing connected vehicles. These guidelines address areas such as data encryption, secure communication, and security monitoring.
- Cybersecurity Audits: Manufacturers must undergo cybersecurity audits to assess compliance with KNCSC regulations. Auditors verify that cybersecurity measures are effective.

6. Other Regions and the Importance of Harmonization

Apart from the aforementioned regions, many other countries are developing or considering automotive cybersecurity regulations. However, there is a growing recognition of the need for harmonization and alignment of global standards to avoid creating barriers to trade and innovation.

Conclusion

Regional regulations and compliance requirements play a critical role in shaping the cybersecurity landscape of the automotive industry. The technical implications of these regulations range from security-by-design principles to risk assessment, incident response, and cybersecurity auditing. As the automotive industry becomes increasingly digital and interconnected, the need for global harmonization of standards becomes more apparent. Manufacturers must navigate a complex web of regulations to ensure their vehicles meet the necessary cybersecurity standards, both at a regional and global level. This harmonization effort is vital to maintain the safety and security of vehicles in an interconnected world.

Chapter 4: Risk Assessment and Threat Modeling

Identifying potential risks and threats

The complex and interconnected nature of modern vehicles, with their digital components and networked systems, has created a challenging landscape for automotive cybersecurity. Identifying potential risks and threats is a fundamental step in safeguarding vehicles and ensuring the safety of drivers and passengers. In this technical exploration, we will delve into the critical processes of risk assessment and threat modeling in the context of automotive cybersecurity, covering the technical details and implications of these practices.

I. Risk Assessment: A Systematic Approach

Risk assessment is a systematic process for identifying, analyzing, and evaluating potential risks within the automotive cybersecurity landscape. It is a proactive measure aimed at preventing and mitigating vulnerabilities and threats that could compromise the security and functionality of a vehicle.

1. Asset Identification

In the context of automotive cybersecurity, assets are the components and systems within a vehicle that need protection. These assets can include:

- Electronic Control Units (ECUs): Identification of the various ECUs that control different vehicle functions, such as the Engine Control Unit (ECU), Transmission Control Unit (TCU), and Body Control Module (BCM).

- Sensors and Actuators: Recognition of sensors (e.g., cameras, lidar, radar) and actuators (e.g., brakes, steering) used for vehicle operations and safety features.
- In-Vehicle Networks: Identification of communication networks like the Controller Area Network (CAN), Local Interconnect Network (LIN), and Ethernet used to transmit data within the vehicle.
- Telematics Systems: Acknowledgment of systems that connect vehicles to external networks for services like remote diagnostics, navigation, and over-the-air (OTA) updates.

2. Threat Identification

After identifying assets, the next step in risk assessment is to identify potential threats that could affect these assets. Threats can be categorized into various types:

- Internal Threats: These originate from within the vehicle and can include software bugs, misconfigurations, and unauthorized access by physical intruders.
- External Threats: These come from external sources and can include remote cyberattacks, data breaches, and malware injection via OTA updates.
- Human Threats: Human errors, negligence, and malicious actions by individuals can also pose threats to automotive cybersecurity.
- Environmental Threats: Natural disasters, extreme temperatures, and physical wear and tear can impact vehicle components.

3. Vulnerability Assessment

Once threats are identified, the assessment process involves understanding vulnerabilities within the vehicle's components and systems. Vulnerabilities are weaknesses that could be exploited by threats.

- Software Vulnerabilities: Examination of the vehicle's software, including the operating system and applications, to identify potential security flaws.
- Hardware Vulnerabilities: Evaluation of the physical hardware components of the vehicle, such as ECUs and sensors, to determine their susceptibility to attacks.
- Network Vulnerabilities: Analysis of the in-vehicle networks and communication protocols to detect potential weaknesses that could be exploited.
- Human-Related Vulnerabilities: Assessment of how human interactions with the vehicle, like user behaviors and access management, can introduce vulnerabilities.

4. Risk Evaluation

After identifying assets, threats, and vulnerabilities, risk evaluation involves assessing the potential impact and likelihood of these risks materializing.

- Impact Assessment: This step evaluates the potential consequences of a risk event. For automotive cybersecurity, impact can range from minor inconveniences to severe safety risks.
- Likelihood Assessment: This assesses how likely it is that a risk event will occur. It takes into account factors like the prevalence of specific threats and the effectiveness of existing security measures.
- Risk Severity: By combining impact and likelihood assessments, the severity of each risk is

determined. This severity ranking helps prioritize the mitigation of risks.

5. Risk Mitigation and Control

Risk mitigation involves implementing measures to reduce the impact and likelihood of identified risks. It includes technical controls, policy implementation, and procedural changes. In the context of automotive cybersecurity, mitigation strategies can include:

- Software Updates: Regularly updating vehicle software to patch vulnerabilities and enhance security.
- Access Controls: Implementing access controls and authentication mechanisms to prevent unauthorized access to vehicle systems.
- Intrusion Detection Systems (IDS): Deploying IDS to monitor and detect anomalous behavior within the vehicle's network.
- Secure Boot Processes: Ensuring that only authenticated and trusted software components are loaded during the vehicle's startup.

II. Threat Modeling: An In-Depth Analysis

Threat modeling is a structured approach to identifying, assessing, and mitigating security threats in a systematic and comprehensive manner. It goes beyond risk assessment by providing detailed insights into specific threats, attack vectors, and potential vulnerabilities within the automotive context.

1. Identifying Assets and Data Flows

Threat modeling begins with identifying the assets and data flows within the vehicle's architecture. This includes understanding how data moves between various components, such as sensors, ECUs, and in-vehicle networks.

- Data Sources: Identifying where data originates, such as sensors and user interfaces.
- Data Destinations: Identifying where data is processed and stored, such as ECUs and in-vehicle storage.
- Data Flow Paths: Mapping how data moves from sources to destinations through in-vehicle networks.

2. Creating a Data Flow Diagram

A data flow diagram visually represents the flow of data within the vehicle's architecture. It illustrates the interconnectedness of various components and data paths.

- External Interfaces: Recognizing external interfaces, such as telematics systems and external communication networks, and understanding how they interact with the vehicle.
- Internal Interfaces: Identifying internal interfaces within the vehicle, such as the communication between ECUs.

3. Identifying Threat Agents and Attack Vectors

In threat modeling, threat agents are entities that have the potential to exploit vulnerabilities. They can be internal or external to the vehicle ecosystem.

- Malicious Actors: Identifying potential threat agents, including cybercriminals, insiders, and even physical intruders.
- Attack Vectors: Analyzing the possible paths or methods that threat agents may use to exploit vulnerabilities and compromise vehicle security.

4. Evaluating Vulnerabilities and Security Controls

Threat modeling requires a detailed evaluation of vulnerabilities and the effectiveness of existing security controls.

- Identifying Vulnerabilities: Recognizing potential weaknesses in the vehicle's software, hardware, and network architecture.
- Analyzing Security Controls: Evaluating the strength of security measures already in place and identifying areas where improvements are needed.

5. Risk Prioritization and Mitigation Planning

Threat modeling involves prioritizing identified threats based on their potential impact and likelihood.

- Risk Prioritization: Determining which threats pose the greatest risk and should be addressed urgently.
- Mitigation Planning: Developing specific strategies and technical measures to mitigate high-priority threats. This can include modifying software, strengthening access controls, and implementing network security measures.

Conclusion

Risk assessment and threat modeling are fundamental technical processes in automotive cybersecurity. These practices help automakers and security professionals identify potential risks and threats, evaluate their impact, and develop mitigation strategies to safeguard vehicles and their occupants. As vehicles become increasingly digital and connected, the need for robust risk assessment and threat modeling processes becomes even more critical. By systematically identifying vulnerabilities and analyzing potential attack vectors, automotive stakeholders can enhance the safety and security of vehicles in an evolving threat landscape.

Strategies for prioritizing security measures

The complexity of modern vehicles, with their intricate digital systems and extensive network connectivity, presents a challenging landscape for automotive cybersecurity. Prioritizing security measures is a crucial step to ensure that resources are allocated effectively to mitigate the most critical threats. In this technical exploration, we will delve into strategies for prioritizing security measures within the context of automotive risk assessment and threat modeling, emphasizing the identification of high-impact threats and the development of targeted mitigation strategies.

I. Identifying High-Impact Threats

The first step in prioritizing security measures is to identify high-impact threats. High-impact threats are those that have the potential to cause significant harm or disruption to the vehicle, its occupants, or external systems. They often target critical vehicle components or sensitive data. Strategies for identifying high-impact threats include:

1. Impact Analysis

Impact analysis involves assessing the potential consequences of a security threat. This analysis helps in determining the level of impact a threat could have on the vehicle, its systems, and its users. Considerations in impact analysis include:

- Safety Implications: Threats that could compromise vehicle safety, such as those affecting braking, steering, or airbag systems, should be considered high-impact.

- Privacy and Data Exposure: Threats that could lead to unauthorized access to sensitive user data, including location information or personal identifiers, are significant.
- Financial Consequences: Threats that could result in substantial financial losses, such as repair costs, recalls, or legal liabilities, are high-impact.

2. Threat Agents and Attack Vectors

Identifying the threat agents and their potential attack vectors is crucial in assessing the impact of threats. Threat agents can be external adversaries, insiders with malicious intent, or even accidental actors. Examining how these agents might exploit vulnerabilities provides insights into potential high-impact scenarios.

- Threat Agent Motivations: Understanding why threat agents might target the vehicle (e.g., financial gain, data theft, or causing harm) helps in assessing impact.
- Attack Vector Severity: Analyzing the sophistication and potential success of attack vectors used by threat agents provides insights into the impact of threats.

3. Attack Surfaces and Vulnerability Assessment

Examining the attack surfaces and associated vulnerabilities within the vehicle architecture is another strategy for identifying high-impact threats. Attack surfaces are areas where the vehicle's systems are exposed to potential threats. Vulnerability assessments help identify weaknesses in these surfaces.

- Critical Vehicle Components: Identifying the most critical components that, if compromised, could lead to severe safety risks.

- Interconnected Systems: Assessing how interconnected vehicle systems can amplify the impact of a threat. For example, an attack on one ECU might affect multiple systems.

II. Strategies for Prioritizing Security Measures

Once high-impact threats are identified, the next step is to prioritize security measures to address these threats effectively. Several strategies can be employed to guide this prioritization process:

1. Risk Severity Assessment

Risk severity assessment combines the impact and likelihood of a threat to determine its overall risk level. A risk matrix can be used to classify threats into categories like low, medium, and high risk. High-risk threats are prioritized for immediate attention.

- Risk Matrices: Using matrices that assign numerical values to impact and likelihood and sum them to derive a risk score.
- Risk Categories: Creating risk categories (e.g., critical, high, medium, low) based on predetermined thresholds.

2. Threat Modeling and Scenario Analysis

Conducting in-depth threat modeling and scenario analysis can help prioritize security measures by simulating potential high-impact threats and their consequences. This process involves:

- Creating Threat Scenarios: Developing detailed scenarios that describe how a high-impact threat might unfold and its potential consequences.
- Impact Assessment: Evaluating the impact of threat scenarios and identifying the specific vehicle

components, systems, and data that would be affected.

- Prioritization based on Scenario Severity: Prioritizing security measures based on the severity of threat scenarios and their potential consequences.

3. Vulnerability Assessment and Testing

Systematic vulnerability assessment and testing can assist in prioritizing security measures by identifying and classifying vulnerabilities. The severity of vulnerabilities can guide prioritization efforts. Key considerations include:

- Vulnerability Scoring: Using standardized scoring systems like the Common Vulnerability Scoring System (CVSS) to rate vulnerabilities.
- Patch Availability: Prioritizing vulnerabilities for which patches or mitigation measures are readily available.
- Exploitation Potential: Assessing the likelihood that a vulnerability will be exploited, especially in high-impact scenarios.

4. Industry and Regulatory Guidance

Industry-specific guidelines and regulatory standards often provide recommendations for prioritizing security measures. Adhering to these standards can assist in ensuring compliance and alignment with best practices.

- ISO/SAE 21434: The standard outlines a structured approach to cybersecurity risk assessment and provides guidance on identifying and mitigating security risks in vehicles.
- UNECE WP.29 and UN Regulation No. 155: These regulations provide specific cybersecurity guidelines

and emphasize the role of independent auditors in assessing cybersecurity measures.

III. Developing Targeted Mitigation Strategies

Once high-impact threats are prioritized, it's essential to develop targeted mitigation strategies to address them effectively. These strategies should align with the specific threats and the associated vulnerabilities and attack vectors. Key considerations for developing mitigation strategies include:

1. Technical Controls

Implementing technical controls is often the primary method of mitigating high-impact threats. These controls can include:

- Software Updates: Regularly patching and updating software to address vulnerabilities.
- Access Controls: Implementing strict access controls and authentication mechanisms to prevent unauthorized access.
- Intrusion Detection Systems (IDS): Deploying IDS to monitor and detect anomalous behavior within the vehicle's network.
- Secure Boot Processes: Ensuring that only authenticated and trusted software components are loaded during the vehicle's startup.

2. Security by Design

Security by design principles should be integrated into the development process, ensuring that security is a consideration from the vehicle's inception.

- Threat Modeling in Development: Incorporating threat modeling as a core component of the development process to identify and address potential high-impact threats early.

- Secure Coding Practices: Ensuring that software is developed with secure coding practices that mitigate known vulnerabilities.

3. Incident Response Planning

Developing an incident response plan that specifically addresses high-impact threats is crucial. This plan should outline how to detect, respond to, and recover from security incidents related to these threats.

4. Continuous Monitoring

Implementing continuous monitoring of the vehicle's cybersecurity landscape is vital for detecting and responding to emerging high-impact threats.

Conclusion

Prioritizing security measures in automotive cybersecurity is a multifaceted process that involves the identification of high-impact threats, the assessment of their potential consequences, and the development of targeted mitigation strategies. As modern vehicles become more complex and digitally connected, it is crucial to focus resources and efforts on addressing the most critical security risks. A systematic approach that combines risk severity assessment, threat modeling, vulnerability assessment, and compliance with industry standards is essential to ensure the safety and security of vehicles and their occupants. By prioritizing security measures effectively, the automotive industry can build trust with consumers and adapt to the evolving threat landscape.

Chapter 5: Security Measures and Best Practices

Secure software development

The increasing complexity of modern vehicles, with their digitally connected systems and autonomous capabilities, has made software development a foundational aspect of automotive cybersecurity. Secure software development ensures that vehicle software is resilient to threats, vulnerabilities are minimized, and data integrity is maintained. In this highly technical exploration, we will delve into secure software development for automotive cybersecurity, focusing on the technical principles and best practices that underpin the process.

I. Understanding the Automotive Software Landscape

Before delving into secure software development, it's important to understand the diverse software components in a modern vehicle. Software in automotive systems is categorized into different types, each with its own set of requirements and potential security challenges. These software categories include:

1. Embedded Software

Embedded software controls various vehicle functions and is directly associated with safety-critical systems. This software is typically stored in Electronic Control Units (ECUs) distributed throughout the vehicle. Key considerations for secure development of embedded software include:

- Safety-Critical Requirements: Adherence to safety standards, such as ISO 26262, to ensure that embedded software does not compromise vehicle safety.

- Real-Time Constraints: Real-time operating systems and determinism are essential for managing critical functions like braking and steering.

2. Infotainment Software

Infotainment software includes the user interfaces, entertainment systems, and connectivity features in the vehicle. While not safety-critical, these systems may access sensitive data, such as personal information and navigation data. Secure development in this context should consider:

- Data Privacy: Protection of user data, including encryption and secure storage of personal information.
- Secure Communication: Ensuring secure communication between infotainment systems and external networks, including over-the-air (OTA) updates.

3. Telematics and Connectivity Software

Telematics systems connect vehicles to external networks, enabling services like remote diagnostics and navigation. These systems are exposed to external threats, making secure development crucial. Considerations include:

- Secure Communication Protocols: Implementing secure communication channels to protect data in transit.
- Authentication and Access Control: Ensuring that only authorized users can access telematics systems.

4. Autonomous Driving Software

Autonomous vehicles rely heavily on software to process sensor data and make driving decisions. The security of this software is paramount to prevent unauthorized control of the vehicle. Key elements for secure autonomous driving software include:

- Safety-Critical Design: Integrating safety and security into the software design to prevent unauthorized access or manipulation of autonomous functions.
- Redundancy and Fail-Safe Mechanisms: Implementing redundancy and fail-safe measures to ensure vehicle safety in case of software failures.

II. Secure Software Development Principles

Secure software development in automotive cybersecurity is based on several fundamental principles that guide the process from design to deployment. These principles are essential to minimize vulnerabilities and ensure the integrity and security of the software.

1. Security by Design

Security should be a fundamental consideration from the beginning of the software development process. This principle entails:

- Threat Modeling: Identifying potential security threats and vulnerabilities specific to the software's context and design.
- Risk Assessment: Assessing the impact and likelihood of identified threats to prioritize security measures.
- Secure Architectural Design: Designing software architectures that separate security-critical functions from non-critical functions and incorporate security controls.

2. Least Privilege and Access Control

The principle of least privilege restricts the access and permissions granted to software components and users. This minimizes the potential damage that can result from a security breach. Access control mechanisms should be enforced at various levels:

- User Access Control: Ensuring that only authorized users have access to specific software functions and data.
- Component Access Control: Limiting the permissions of software components and ECUs to only the actions they require.

3. Secure Development Frameworks and Libraries

Using established secure development frameworks, libraries, and best practices is critical to avoiding common vulnerabilities. These frameworks provide pre-built solutions for security challenges, including:

- Secure Coding Standards: Adherence to secure coding standards such as CERT C and ISO/IEC 27034 for embedded systems.
- Vulnerability Scanners: Utilizing tools that automatically detect and report common vulnerabilities in code.

III. Secure Coding Practices

Secure coding practices are the core of secure software development. These practices address the specific coding techniques that help identify and mitigate vulnerabilities. Key elements of secure coding practices include:

1. Input Validation and Sanitization

Insecure handling of user input is a common source of vulnerabilities. Input validation and sanitization ensure that input data is verified and cleaned before being processed. Practices include:

- Whitelisting: Allowing only known, safe input and blocking all other data.
- Sanitization: Cleaning and validating input to ensure it adheres to expected formats.

2. Secure Memory Management

Memory-related vulnerabilities, such as buffer overflows and use-after-free errors, can be exploited by attackers. Secure memory management practices include:

- Buffer Overflow Protection: Ensuring that buffer sizes are checked to prevent overflow.
- Safe Memory Allocation: Using safe memory allocation functions to prevent memory-related vulnerabilities.

3. Authentication and Authorization Controls

Authentication ensures that users are who they claim to be, while authorization controls dictate what actions users are allowed to perform. Secure coding practices in this area include:

- Strong Password Hashing: Using cryptographic hashing algorithms to securely store and validate passwords.
- Role-Based Access Control (RBAC): Implementing RBAC to define and enforce user permissions.

4. Encryption

Data encryption is essential to protect sensitive information from unauthorized access. Secure coding practices for encryption include:

- Symmetric and Asymmetric Encryption: Using appropriate encryption methods for data in transit and data at rest.

- Key Management: Securely managing encryption keys to prevent unauthorized decryption.

5. Error Handling and Logging

Secure error handling and logging practices are crucial for diagnosing and responding to security incidents. These practices include:

- Limited Error Information: Restricting the amount of error information exposed to users or attackers.
- Secure Logging: Ensuring that log entries are handled securely and are not accessible to unauthorized users.

IV. Secure Testing and Verification

Secure software development is incomplete without rigorous testing and verification. The goal is to identify and address security vulnerabilities before software is deployed. Key testing and verification strategies include:

1. Static Analysis

Static code analysis involves examining source code or binary code without executing it. This technique can uncover potential vulnerabilities and coding errors.

- Static Analysis Tools: Using specialized static analysis tools to identify security vulnerabilities.
- Code Review: Manual code review to detect security issues that automated tools may miss.

2. Dynamic Analysis

Dynamic analysis involves examining code during runtime to identify vulnerabilities that might not be evident in the source code.

- Dynamic Scanners: Employing dynamic scanning tools to discover runtime vulnerabilities, such as input validation issues or memory leaks.

- Penetration Testing: Actively probing software systems to identify vulnerabilities by simulating real-world attacks.

3. Fuzz Testing

Fuzz testing involves sending unexpected, invalid, or random data inputs to software components to discover vulnerabilities.

- Fuzzing Tools: Using fuzzing tools and techniques to systematically test software for unexpected behaviors and vulnerabilities.

4. Security Regression Testing

Regular regression testing focuses on ensuring that security fixes and patches do not introduce new vulnerabilities.

V. Secure Deployment and Maintenance

Secure software development extends to deployment and ongoing maintenance. Key practices for secure deployment and maintenance include:

1. Secure Configuration Management

Configurations should be managed securely to minimize vulnerabilities and ensure consistent security across software deployments.

- Secure Defaults: Implementing secure default configurations for software components.
- Configuration Auditing: Regularly auditing configurations to detect unauthorized changes.

2. Patch Management

Software patches and updates should be applied promptly to address known vulnerabilities and security issues.

- Patch Management Process: Implementing a structured process for identifying, testing, and deploying patches.

- Vulnerability Scanning: Regularly scanning software for known vulnerabilities.

3. Incident Response

Having a well-defined incident response plan is crucial for addressing security incidents. The plan should outline how to detect, respond to, and recover from security incidents.

- Security Incident Team: Establishing a dedicated team responsible for handling security incidents.
- Response Protocols: Developing documented protocols for responding to various types of security incidents.

4. Secure Software Lifecycle Management

A secure software development lifecycle (SDLC) integrates security throughout all phases of software development, from design to deployment and maintenance. This approach ensures that security remains a core consideration at every stage of the development process.

Conclusion

Secure software development is a complex and multifaceted process that plays a critical role in automotive cybersecurity. As vehicles become more reliant on software for their operation, the need for robust and comprehensive security practices becomes paramount. Integrating security from the design phase, employing secure coding practices, and implementing thorough testing and verification processes are essential to create secure software for vehicles. By following the technical principles and best practices outlined in this discussion, the automotive industry can maintain the safety and security of vehicles in an ever-evolving digital landscape.

Secure communication protocols

In modern vehicles, secure communication is vital for ensuring the confidentiality, integrity, and availability of data as it traverses various networks and interfaces. The diverse communication needs of vehicles, including in-vehicle networks, external connectivity, and over-the-air (OTA) updates, require robust security measures. This technical exploration delves into secure communication protocols for automotive cybersecurity, emphasizing the technical principles and best practices that underpin these protocols.

I. Understanding Automotive Communication Challenges

Before diving into secure communication protocols, it's crucial to understand the unique communication challenges faced by vehicles. These challenges stem from the multifaceted nature of automotive communication, which encompasses various networks and interfaces:

1. In-Vehicle Networks

Modern vehicles feature several in-vehicle networks for different purposes, including the Controller Area Network (CAN), Local Interconnect Network (LIN), and Ethernet. These networks must securely transmit data between electronic control units (ECUs) while preventing unauthorized access and tampering.

2. Telematics and Connectivity

Telematics systems connect vehicles to external networks, enabling features like remote diagnostics, navigation, and infotainment. Ensuring secure connectivity between the vehicle and external services is essential.

3. Over-the-Air (OTA) Updates

OTA updates have become a common method for deploying software and firmware updates to vehicles.

Secure OTA updates are necessary to prevent malicious interference and ensure the integrity of updates.

II. Secure Communication Protocol Principles

Secure communication protocols in the automotive context are guided by a set of fundamental principles that prioritize data security and privacy:

1. Confidentiality

Confidentiality ensures that data remains protected from unauthorized access. This principle involves encrypting data to ensure that only authorized entities can decipher it. Key considerations include:

- Data Encryption: Implementing strong encryption algorithms to protect data in transit and at rest.
- Key Management: Securely managing encryption keys to prevent unauthorized access.

2. Integrity

Integrity guarantees that data remains unaltered during transmission. Detecting any unauthorized modifications or tampering with data is essential. Key aspects of data integrity include:

- Message Authentication Codes (MACs): Using MACs to verify the integrity of data and detect unauthorized changes.
- Digital Signatures: Employing digital signatures to verify the authenticity and integrity of data.

3. Authentication

Authentication verifies the identity of the communicating parties. Ensuring that data is exchanged between legitimate entities is critical. Authentication methods include:

- Mutual Authentication: Verifying the identity of both the sender and the recipient.

- Digital Certificates: Employing digital certificates to confirm the authenticity of entities.

4. Access Control

Access control mechanisms define who is allowed to send and receive data and what actions they are permitted to perform. These mechanisms restrict access to authorized entities only. Best practices for access control include:

- Role-Based Access Control (RBAC): Implementing RBAC to define and enforce user permissions.
- Access Control Lists (ACLs): Using ACLs to specify which entities can access specific data or services.

5. Secure Key Exchange

Secure key exchange mechanisms facilitate the establishment of secure communication channels. Ensuring that keys are exchanged securely and that they remain confidential is essential. Techniques include:

- Diffie-Hellman Key Exchange: Employing Diffie-Hellman or Ephemeral Diffie-Hellman for secure key exchange.
- Pre-Shared Keys (PSKs): Using pre-shared keys for authentication and key establishment.

III. Secure Communication Protocols and Best Practices

Secure communication protocols for vehicles encompass a range of technical measures and best practices to protect data during transmission. Let's explore these measures in detail:

1. Transport Layer Security (TLS) for Secure Data Exchange

TLS is a widely used protocol for securing data transmission over networks. In the automotive context, it can be employed for securing communication between in-vehicle ECUs, telematics systems, and external servers.

- Certificate-Based Authentication: Use digital certificates to verify the identities of entities involved in the communication.
- Data Encryption: Employ strong encryption ciphers (e.g., AES) to protect data from eavesdropping.
- Perfect Forward Secrecy (PFS): Implement PFS to ensure that even if one session's encryption keys are compromised, past and future sessions remain secure.

2. Secure In-Vehicle Network Protocols

In-vehicle networks like CAN and LIN require specialized protocols to ensure secure communication within the vehicle. Key best practices include:

- Message Authentication: Implement message authentication codes (MACs) to verify the integrity of messages on the network.
- Access Control: Enforce access controls and authentication mechanisms to restrict access to in-vehicle networks.

3. Secure Telematics Protocols

Telematics systems are the gateway to external networks and services. Securing this interface is essential. Best practices for telematics protocols include:

- Secure Tunneling: Establish secure tunnels, such as Virtual Private Networks (VPNs), to protect data in transit.
- Secure Boot Processes: Ensure that telematics systems boot securely and that only authenticated and trusted software components are loaded during startup.

4. Secure OTA Update Protocols

OTA updates have become a critical method for deploying software and firmware updates to vehicles. Best practices for secure OTA updates include:

- Code Signing: Employ digital signatures to verify the authenticity and integrity of updates.
- Secure Channels: Use secure channels, such as TLS, for the transmission of update packages.
- Rollback Protection: Implement mechanisms to prevent attackers from downgrading the vehicle's software to a vulnerable version.

5. Intrusion Detection and Prevention Systems (IDS/IPS)

Intrusion detection and prevention systems play a crucial role in identifying and responding to security threats. Best practices include:

- Real-Time Monitoring: Continuously monitor network traffic and system behavior for anomalies and potential intrusions.
- Alerts and Response: Set up automated alerts and response mechanisms to address detected threats promptly.

IV. Compliance with Industry Standards

Automotive cybersecurity standards and regulations, such as ISO/SAE 21434 and UN Regulation No. 155, provide guidelines for secure communication protocols in vehicles. Compliance with these standards is crucial for ensuring alignment with industry best practices and legal requirements.

Conclusion

Secure communication protocols are the backbone of automotive cybersecurity, ensuring that data is transmitted and received securely within and outside the vehicle. The technical principles and best practices outlined in this discussion are fundamental to safeguarding the confidentiality, integrity, and availability of data in modern vehicles. As vehicles continue to evolve with increased connectivity and automation, the importance of robust secure communication protocols becomes even more pronounced. By adhering to these technical principles and best practices, the automotive industry can build trust with consumers and enhance the security of vehicles in an ever-connected world.

Intrusion detection systems

Intrusion Detection Systems (IDS) play a pivotal role in the automotive cybersecurity landscape, helping safeguard modern vehicles from unauthorized access, cyberattacks, and intrusions. In this in-depth technical exploration, we will delve into the intricacies of IDS in the context of automotive cybersecurity, examining key principles, best practices, and the technical aspects that underpin their operation.

I. Understanding the Automotive Intrusion Detection Landscape

Before diving into the technical details of IDS in the automotive sector, it's essential to comprehend the specific challenges and nuances that the automotive industry faces in the realm of intrusion detection.

Diverse Attack Surfaces: Modern vehicles feature a wide array of electronic control units (ECUs), networks, and interfaces, creating diverse attack surfaces that adversaries can exploit.

Complex Vehicle Architecture: The complexity of automotive systems necessitates a systematic approach to intrusion detection, where a multitude of interconnected components and communication protocols must be considered.

Safety-Critical Systems: Intrusion detection in vehicles must balance security needs with safety-critical functions. A false positive or negative in an IDS can have severe implications for vehicle safety.

II. Principles and Categories of IDS

Intrusion Detection Systems in the automotive context adhere to several fundamental principles that dictate their operation. IDS can be categorized into two primary types:

Signature-Based IDS:

- Principle: Signature-based IDS identifies intrusions by comparing observed patterns in network traffic or system behavior to known attack signatures.
- Technical Elements: Signature databases, pattern matching algorithms, and anomaly detection mechanisms.

Anomaly-Based IDS:

- Principle: Anomaly-based IDS identifies intrusions by flagging deviations from established baselines of normal behavior. These deviations may indicate malicious activity.
- Technical Elements: Statistical models, machine learning algorithms, and baseline generation techniques.

III. Deploying IDS in Vehicles

The deployment of IDS in vehicles involves several technical considerations, ensuring that the system is capable of detecting intrusions effectively and efficiently.

Sensors and Data Sources:

- IDS in vehicles rely on data from various sensors, ECUs, and network traffic for intrusion detection.
- Technical aspects include data capture, processing, and aggregation.

Real-Time Monitoring:

- IDS must operate in real-time to detect intrusions as they occur.
- Technical challenges encompass low-latency processing and timely response mechanisms.

Resource Constraints:

- Vehicles have limited computational resources, which impact the design and implementation of IDS.
- Lightweight algorithms, efficient memory usage, and optimized processing are essential.

Integration with Vehicle Networks:

- IDS must seamlessly integrate with in-vehicle networks like CAN, LIN, and Ethernet.
- Technical aspects include protocol compatibility and monitoring techniques.

IV. Signature-Based IDS in Automotive Cybersecurity

Signature-based IDS relies on known attack patterns to identify intrusions. In the automotive context, it involves creating and maintaining signature databases specific to the vehicle's architecture and communication protocols.

Signature Development:

- Creating and updating signatures that describe known attack patterns and vulnerabilities.
- Technical elements include pattern description, regular expressions, and attack signature management.

Pattern Matching:
- Pattern matching algorithms compare observed data to known signatures to identify intrusions.
- Technical aspects include algorithms like Aho-Corasick and efficient pattern matching techniques.

Protocol and ECU-Specific Signatures:
- Automotive signature-based IDS must account for the unique protocols and ECUs used in vehicles.
- Technical expertise in understanding and defining signatures for automotive communication protocols.

V. Anomaly-Based IDS in Automotive Cybersecurity

Anomaly-based IDS, in contrast to signature-based IDS, relies on identifying deviations from normal behavior. These deviations may indicate intrusions or irregularities.

Baseline Generation:
- Anomaly-based IDS create baselines of normal behavior by analyzing historical data.
- Technical elements include statistical modeling, machine learning algorithms, and feature selection techniques.

Machine Learning for Anomaly Detection:

- Machine learning algorithms, such as clustering and classification models, are applied to detect anomalies.
- Technical details involve algorithm selection, model training, and feature engineering.

Adaptive Learning:

- Anomaly-based IDS adapt their baselines to account for changes in normal behavior over time.
- Technical challenges encompass dynamic baseline adjustment and adaptive learning algorithms.

VI. Network Intrusion Detection in Vehicles

Network intrusion detection is a critical component of automotive IDS, focusing on securing in-vehicle networks and external connectivity.

CAN Bus Monitoring:

- The Controller Area Network (CAN) is a common target for attacks; IDS must monitor and protect this network.
- Technical considerations include message validation, ECU behavior analysis, and message timing analysis.

Telematics and Connectivity:

- Telematics systems connect vehicles to external networks, making them a potential entry point for attackers.
- Technical aspects involve secure tunneling, data encryption, and secure communication protocols.

Over-the-Air (OTA) Updates:

- IDS must ensure the integrity of OTA updates to prevent malicious interference.
- Technical considerations encompass code signing, secure channels for update delivery, and rollback protection.

VII. Host-Based Intrusion Detection in Vehicles

Host-based intrusion detection focuses on individual ECUs and systems within the vehicle, identifying intrusions and irregularities at the ECU level.

ECU Monitoring:
- IDS must continuously monitor the behavior and communication of individual ECUs.
- Technical aspects include sensor data analysis, protocol-specific monitoring, and anomaly detection at the ECU level.

Operating System Security:
- Intrusion detection in vehicles extends to the security of ECU operating systems.
- Technical elements involve OS hardening, security patch management, and kernel-level monitoring.

VIII. Technical Challenges and Best Practices

Intrusion detection in vehicles presents unique technical challenges, and addressing these challenges requires specific best practices:

Real-Time Processing:
- The need for real-time intrusion detection poses challenges in terms of low-latency processing and efficient algorithms.
- Technical solutions involve optimized code and hardware acceleration.

Resource-Efficient Algorithms:

- Vehicles have limited computational resources, necessitating the use of resource-efficient intrusion detection algorithms.
- Technical best practices include algorithm optimization and memory management.

Communication Protocol Expertise:
- Understanding the intricacies of automotive communication protocols is crucial for effective intrusion detection.
- Technical expertise includes protocol analysis and knowledge of message formats.

Regular Updates:
- IDS must be regularly updated to account for new attack patterns and vulnerabilities.
- Technical practices encompass efficient update mechanisms and version control.

IX. Incident Response and Mitigation

IDS play a central role in incident detection, but the response and mitigation strategies are equally vital.

Alerting and Notification:
- IDS should generate alerts and notifications for detected intrusions.
- Technical aspects involve alert formats, escalation processes, and notification protocols.

Response Mechanisms:
- IDS should integrate with incident response mechanisms to initiate timely and effective responses to intrusions.

- Technical considerations include response automation and incident handling procedures.

X. Compliance with Automotive Cybersecurity Standards

Compliance with automotive cybersecurity standards, such as ISO/SAE 21434 and UN Regulation No. 155, is essential for ensuring that IDS in vehicles align with industry best practices and regulatory requirements.

XI. Conclusion

Intrusion Detection Systems (IDS) are critical components of automotive cybersecurity, helping protect vehicles from unauthorized access and cyberattacks. Their technical intricacies encompass a range of principles, deployment considerations, and best practices tailored to the automotive landscape. As vehicles continue to evolve with increased connectivity and automation, the role of IDS in ensuring automotive cybersecurity becomes even more pronounced. By adhering to the technical principles and best practices outlined in this discussion, the automotive industry can enhance the security and trustworthiness of vehicles in an ever-connected digital world.

Chapter 6: Secure Vehicle Architecture

Hardware security modules

In the realm of automotive cybersecurity, hardware security modules (HSMs) are critical components that play a vital role in safeguarding modern vehicles against cyber threats. This extensive technical exploration delves into the intricacies of HSMs in the context of automotive cybersecurity, examining key principles, best practices, and the technical aspects that underpin their operation.

I. Understanding the Role of Hardware Security Modules in Automotive Cybersecurity

Before we dive into the technical aspects of HSMs, it's crucial to grasp the significance of these specialized hardware components in the context of automotive cybersecurity.

Hardware Root of Trust: HSMs serve as the hardware root of trust in the vehicle's architecture, providing a foundation for secure operations.

Cryptographic Operations: HSMs are responsible for cryptographic key management, secure storage, and the execution of security-critical operations, such as encryption and digital signature generation.

Protection against Physical Attacks: HSMs are designed to resist physical tampering, ensuring the confidentiality and integrity of cryptographic keys and sensitive data.

II. Principles and Functional Categories of HSMs

Hardware Security Modules adhere to several fundamental principles that dictate their operation. HSMs can be categorized into two primary functional categories:

Embedded HSMs:

- Principle: Embedded HSMs are integrated directly into electronic control units (ECUs) within the vehicle. They provide localized security features tailored to specific ECUs.
- Technical Aspects: Integration into ECUs, hardware-based cryptography, and secure storage.

Centralized HSMs:

- Principle: Centralized HSMs are separate modules that provide security services to multiple ECUs and systems within the vehicle architecture.
- Technical Aspects: Secure communication with ECUs, role-based access control, and secure key management.

III. Secure Vehicle Key Management with HSMs

Key management is a core function of HSMs in automotive cybersecurity. Managing cryptographic keys securely is essential to protect data and communications within the vehicle.

Key Generation:

- Technical Elements: True random number generation, secure key pair creation, and entropy sources.

Key Storage:

- Technical Aspects: Secure key storage, anti-tamper mechanisms, and encrypted key containers.

Key Usage:

- Technical Practices: Secure cryptographic operations, key distribution, and key revocation.

Key Lifecycle Management:
- Technical Considerations: Key rotation, backup and recovery, and secure key deletion.

IV. Cryptographic Operations and Protocols in HSMs

HSMs are responsible for executing cryptographic operations securely, underpinning the confidentiality and integrity of data and communications within the vehicle.

Encryption and Decryption:
- Technical Elements: Symmetric and asymmetric encryption algorithms, encryption modes, and hardware acceleration.

Digital Signatures:
- Technical Aspects: Digital signature algorithms, key management for signatures, and secure hashing.

Secure Protocols:
- Technical Practices: Implementing secure communication protocols, such as Transport Layer Security (TLS) and Secure Sockets Layer (SSL).

V. Protection against Physical Attacks

HSMs are designed to resist physical tampering and attacks. Ensuring the security and integrity of HSMs under physical assault is a critical aspect of automotive cybersecurity.

Secure Enclosures:

- Technical Features: Tamper-evident and tamper-resistant enclosures, anti-drilling measures, and intrusion detection sensors.

Anti-Tamper Mechanisms:
- Technical Practices: Active response mechanisms, including self-destruct features, and passive response measures, such as shielding.

Secure Boot Processes:
- Technical Elements: Verified boot processes, secure code execution, and cryptographic measurement.

VI. Embedded HSMs in Vehicle Architecture

Embedded HSMs are integrated directly into ECUs within the vehicle, providing localized security features tailored to specific functions.

ECU Integration:
- Technical Details: Integration of embedded HSMs into safety-critical ECUs, infotainment systems, and telematics units.

Secure Communication:
- Technical Aspects: Establishing secure communication channels between embedded HSMs and other ECUs.

Secure Storage:
- Technical Elements: Secure storage of cryptographic keys and sensitive data within embedded HSMs.

Key Management within ECUs:
- Technical Practices: Managing cryptographic keys within embedded HSMs for specific ECU functions.

VII. Centralized HSMs for Vehicle-Wide Security

Centralized HSMs, as separate modules, provide security services to multiple ECUs and systems within the vehicle architecture.

Interoperability with ECUs:
- Technical Challenges: Ensuring centralized HSMs can securely interact with various ECUs across the vehicle.

Role-Based Access Control:
- Technical Aspects: Implementing RBAC mechanisms to define and enforce user permissions.

Secure Communication with ECUs:
- Technical Practices: Establishing secure channels for communication between centralized HSMs and ECUs.

Secure Key Management:
- Technical Details: Managing cryptographic keys securely within centralized HSMs and distributing them to authorized ECUs.

VIII. Secure OTA Updates with HSMs

Over-the-Air (OTA) updates have become a common method for deploying software and firmware updates to vehicles. HSMs play a crucial role in ensuring the integrity and authenticity of these updates.

Code Signing and Verification:
- Technical Elements: Employing digital signatures to verify the authenticity and integrity of OTA updates.

Secure Channels:

- Technical Practices: Using secure channels, such as Transport Layer Security (TLS), for the transmission of OTA update packages.

Rollback Protection:
- Technical Aspects: Implementing mechanisms to prevent attackers from downgrading the vehicle's software to a vulnerable version.

IX. Compliance with Automotive Cybersecurity Standards

Compliance with automotive cybersecurity standards and regulations, such as ISO/SAE 21434 and UN Regulation No. 155, is crucial to ensure that HSMs in vehicles align with industry best practices and legal requirements.

X. Conclusion

Hardware Security Modules (HSMs) are indispensable components in automotive cybersecurity, serving as the hardware root of trust and facilitating secure operations, cryptographic key management, and protection against physical attacks. The technical principles and best practices outlined in this discussion underscore the pivotal role of HSMs in ensuring the security and trustworthiness of modern vehicles in an ever-connected digital world. As vehicles continue to evolve with increased connectivity and automation, the importance of robust HSMs becomes even more pronounced, highlighting their central role in the secure architecture of vehicles. By adhering to the technical principles and best practices outlined here, the automotive industry can build trust with consumers and enhance the security of vehicles in the evolving landscape of automotive cybersecurity.

Secure boot processes

In the complex landscape of automotive cybersecurity, secure boot processes play a pivotal role in ensuring the integrity and trustworthiness of vehicle systems. This detailed technical exploration delves into the intricacies of secure boot processes within the context of automotive cybersecurity, covering key principles, best practices, and the technical aspects underpinning their implementation.

I. The Importance of Secure Boot Processes in Automotive Cybersecurity

Before delving into the technical aspects of secure boot processes, it's crucial to understand their significance in safeguarding the integrity of vehicle systems.

> Root of Trust: Secure boot processes establish a root of trust that ensures that the vehicle's software components, from the bootloader to the operating system, are authentic and untampered.

> Protection Against Malware: Secure boot prevents malicious or unauthorized software from gaining control over the vehicle's systems, ensuring that only trusted code is executed.

> Safety-Critical Systems: In the context of automotive cybersecurity, secure boot is particularly critical for safety-critical systems, as any compromise could have life-threatening consequences.

II. Principles and Components of Secure Boot Processes

Secure boot processes follow a set of fundamental principles to guarantee the integrity of the boot sequence. The components of secure boot include:

> Bootloader Integrity:

- Principle: The bootloader is the first piece of code executed on boot and must be cryptographically verified to ensure its integrity.
- Technical Elements: Cryptographic signatures, secure storage of bootloader code, and anti-rollback protection.

Chain of Trust:

- Principle: Secure boot establishes a chain of trust, ensuring that each subsequent component in the boot process is verified before execution.
- Technical Aspects: Measurement of code integrity, secure handover of control, and trust anchor establishment.

Secure Storage:

- Principle: The secure storage of cryptographic keys and measurement values is essential to prevent tampering.
- Technical Practices: Secure storage hardware, secure key management, and anti-tamper mechanisms.

Verified Boot Sequence:

- Principle: The boot sequence must be validated to confirm that each component is unaltered and authentic.
- Technical Considerations: Cryptographic verification of boot components, including the operating system and critical applications.

III. Secure Boot Processes for Embedded ECUs

Embedded ECUs within vehicles rely on secure boot processes to ensure that only trusted code is executed. The technical aspects of secure boot for embedded ECUs include:

Measurement and Attestation:
- Technical Elements: Measuring code and system integrity during boot, and providing attestation evidence to a trusted authority.

Secure Handover:
- Technical Practices: Secure handover of control from one component to another, ensuring that control is not seized by malicious code.

Cryptographic Signatures:
- Technical Details: Cryptographically signing code and measurement values to verify their authenticity.

Root of Trust:
- Technical Aspects: Establishing a hardware-based root of trust to anchor the secure boot process.

IV. Secure Boot Processes for Infotainment Systems

Infotainment systems, while less safety-critical, are essential components in modern vehicles. Secure boot processes for infotainment systems include:

Code Signing:
- Technical Practices: Employing digital signatures to verify the authenticity and integrity of infotainment software components.

Secure Communication:

- Technical Considerations: Ensuring secure communication between infotainment systems and external sources, such as over-the-air (OTA) updates.

Secure Boot Extensions:
- Technical Elements: Extending secure boot processes to infotainment systems to cover user-facing functionalities.

User Authentication:
- Technical Aspects: Securely authenticating users before allowing access to infotainment functions.

V. Secure Boot Processes for Telematics and Connectivity

Telematics systems provide connectivity to external networks, making secure boot processes vital in ensuring secure connections and preventing unauthorized access:

Secure Network Establishment:
- Technical Practices: Establishing secure network connections to external services and ensuring secure data transmission.

Digital Certificates:
- Technical Elements: Employing digital certificates for secure authentication and communication with external servers.

Secure Boot for OTA Updates:
- Technical Considerations: Extending secure boot processes to cover OTA updates and ensuring the integrity of incoming updates.

Remote Attestation:
- Technical Aspects: Performing remote attestation to confirm the security and

integrity of telematics systems to external authorities.

VI. Challenges and Best Practices

Secure boot processes in automotive cybersecurity pose unique technical challenges, and addressing these challenges requires specific best practices:

Hardware-Based Security:

- Technical Solutions: Implementing secure hardware components, such as Hardware Security Modules (HSMs), for cryptographic operations and key management.

Cryptographic Techniques:

- Technical Best Practices: Employing strong cryptographic algorithms and practices for code signing, key generation, and secure storage.

Firmware Updates:

- Technical Challenges: Managing firmware updates effectively while maintaining the integrity of the boot process.

Anti-Tamper Mechanisms:

- Technical Considerations: Implementing anti-tamper features to resist physical attacks on the boot process.

VII. Secure Boot Processes and Industry Standards

Compliance with automotive cybersecurity standards, such as ISO/SAE 21434 and UN Regulation No. 155, is crucial to ensure that secure boot processes in vehicles align with industry best practices and legal requirements.

VIII. Conclusion

Secure boot processes are the cornerstone of automotive cybersecurity, ensuring that only trusted and authentic code is executed during the vehicle's boot sequence. The technical principles and best practices outlined in this discussion highlight the critical role of secure boot processes in securing the integrity of vehicle systems. In an era of increasing connectivity and automation, the need for robust and well-implemented secure boot processes becomes even more pronounced. By adhering to the technical principles and best practices outlined here, the automotive industry can enhance the security and trustworthiness of vehicles in the evolving landscape of automotive cybersecurity.

Secure over-the-air (OTA) updates

In the rapidly evolving landscape of automotive technology, over-the-air (OTA) updates have emerged as a pivotal method for enhancing vehicle functionality, fixing software bugs, and addressing security vulnerabilities. However, with this convenience comes the need for robust security measures to ensure that OTA updates do not become vectors for cyberattacks. This technical exploration delves into the intricacies of securing OTA updates within the context of automotive cybersecurity, covering key principles, best practices, and the technical aspects that underpin their implementation.

I. Introduction

The integration of OTA updates into modern vehicles is a significant leap forward in terms of convenience and efficiency. This capability allows automakers to deliver software and firmware updates remotely, reducing the need for physical service visits. However, securing OTA updates is paramount to safeguard against potential threats.

II. The Significance of OTA Update Security

OTA updates are not without their risks, as they introduce potential attack vectors if not adequately protected. The significance of OTA update security lies in:

> Mitigating Malicious Updates: Ensuring that only authorized and legitimate updates are applied to the vehicle's software.
>
> Preventing Unauthorized Access: Protecting the communication channels used for OTA updates from unauthorized access and eavesdropping.
>
> Maintaining Vehicle Safety: OTA updates must not compromise the safety-critical functions of the vehicle.

III. Principles and Best Practices for OTA Update Security

Securing OTA updates is founded on a set of core principles and best practices:

> Code Signing and Verification:
>
> - Principle: Digitally sign OTA updates to confirm their authenticity and integrity.
> - Technical Aspects: Employing digital signatures using cryptographic keys, verification mechanisms, and secure code repositories.
>
> Secure Channels:
>
> - Principle: Establishing secure communication channels for transmitting OTA updates.
> - Technical Considerations: Implementing secure protocols like Transport Layer

Security (TLS) for encryption and secure data transmission.

Rollback Protection:

- Principle: Preventing attackers from downgrading the vehicle's software to a vulnerable version.
- Technical Elements: Version control, secure update storage, and verification of update integrity.

Secure Boot Processes:

- Principle: Ensuring that the vehicle securely boots into the updated software after an OTA update.
- Technical Practices: Implementing secure boot processes, cryptographic verification, and secure handover of control.

IV. Secure Code Signing and Verification

Code signing is a fundamental aspect of OTA update security. It involves digitally signing the update package and verifying the signature to confirm the update's authenticity.

Digital Signatures:

- Technical Details: Generating digital signatures using cryptographic algorithms like RSA or ECDSA and securely storing the private signing keys.

Key Management:

- Technical Aspects: Securely managing the cryptographic keys used for code signing, including key generation, storage, and rotation.

Signature Verification:

- Technical Practices: Implementing the verification of digital signatures during the update process to confirm the update's authenticity and integrity.

V. Establishing Secure Communication Channels

Securing the communication channels used for OTA updates is critical to protect against eavesdropping and unauthorized access.

Transport Layer Security (TLS):

- Technical Considerations: Implementing TLS protocols to ensure encrypted and authenticated communication between the update server and the vehicle.

Mutual Authentication:

- Technical Practices: Employing mutual authentication between the vehicle and the update server, verifying the identities of both parties.

Secure Tunneling:

- Technical Elements: Establishing secure tunnels, such as Virtual Private Networks (VPNs), for transmitting OTA updates securely.

VI. Preventing Rollback Attacks

Rollback attacks, where an attacker downgrades the software to a previously vulnerable version, are a significant threat to OTA update security.

Version Control:

- Technical Aspects: Implementing version control mechanisms that prevent the installation of older or unauthorized updates.

Secure Update Storage:

- Technical Practices: Securely storing update packages on the vehicle to prevent tampering and unauthorized access.

Update Integrity Verification:
- Technical Details: Verifying the integrity of an update's code and data to detect unauthorized modifications.

VII. Secure Boot Processes for OTA Updates

The secure boot process ensures that the vehicle securely boots into the updated software after an OTA update. This is a technical aspect that requires careful implementation.

Verified Boot Sequence:
- Technical Elements: Cryptographically verifying the integrity and authenticity of boot components, including the updated software.

Secure Handover:
- Technical Practices: Securely handing over control from the old software to the updated version, preventing any interruptions or attacks during the process.

VIII. Compliance with Automotive Cybersecurity Standards

Compliance with automotive cybersecurity standards and regulations, such as ISO/SAE 21434 and UN Regulation No. 155, is essential to ensure that OTA updates in vehicles align with industry best practices and legal requirements.

IX. Conclusion

Securing OTA updates is a paramount aspect of automotive cybersecurity in an age of increasing connectivity and software-driven vehicle systems. By adhering to the technical principles and best practices outlined in this discussion, the automotive industry can mitigate the risks associated with OTA updates and enhance the security and trustworthiness of vehicles in an ever-connected digital world. As OTA updates become more prevalent, robust security measures are indispensable to maintain the integrity of the vehicle's software and protect against potential cyber threats.

Chapter 7: Incident Response and Recovery

Steps to take during a cyber incident

In the realm of automotive cybersecurity, the management of cyber incidents is of paramount importance. As vehicles become more connected and reliant on electronic systems, the risk of cyber threats has grown significantly. In this comprehensive technical discussion, we will explore the essential steps to be taken during a cyber incident in the automotive industry. These steps are crucial for identifying, managing, and recovering from cyber threats that could impact the safety, functionality, and data security of connected vehicles.

I. Introduction

The automotive industry is undergoing a digital transformation, with vehicles becoming increasingly connected and reliant on electronic control systems. This digital evolution has created new opportunities but also introduced cybersecurity risks. Effective incident response and recovery processes are essential to safeguard both vehicle and driver safety. In this discussion, we will focus on the technical steps involved in handling cyber incidents in the automotive sector.

II. Incident Identification

> Anomaly Detection: The incident response process starts with the detection of anomalies or suspicious activities within the vehicle's electronic systems. Anomalies can be identified through various means, including intrusion detection systems, anomaly-based detection algorithms, and continuous monitoring of vehicle network traffic.

Alert Triage: Security teams review and prioritize the alerts generated by detection systems. Alerts are categorized based on their severity and potential impact on vehicle safety and operation.

Forensic Data Collection: Gathering digital evidence is crucial. The collection of forensic data, including log files, network packet captures, and system snapshots, enables investigators to reconstruct the incident's timeline and understand its origins.

III. Incident Containment

Isolation of Affected Systems: Upon confirming an incident, the immediate priority is to isolate the affected systems to prevent the threat from spreading further. This is achieved through network segmentation and, in some cases, physically disconnecting the affected component from the vehicle's network.

Mitigation: Strategies are implemented to mitigate the impact of the incident. This may include disabling compromised functions, blocking network communication to specific components, and applying security patches or updates.

Preserving Evidence: It is essential to preserve evidence for further analysis and potential legal action. Investigators ensure that incident-related data and artifacts are safeguarded from alteration.

IV. Incident Eradication

Root Cause Analysis: A deep technical analysis is conducted to determine the root cause of the incident. This analysis helps identify the vulnerabilities, weaknesses, or misconfigurations that led to the breach.

Vulnerability Remediation: Based on the root cause analysis, vulnerabilities are addressed. This may involve software patching, firmware updates, or configuration changes to eliminate the vulnerabilities exploited by the attacker.

Password Resets: If the incident involved unauthorized access or compromised user accounts, all affected accounts are reset. Multifactor authentication (MFA) may be enforced to enhance account security.

V. Data Recovery

Data Backups: Data recovery often involves restoring information from backups. Regular, secure backups are crucial to ensure that data can be recovered without significant data loss. This step is particularly important for preserving critical data, such as telematics data or driver profiles.

Data Integrity Checks: Recovered data is carefully validated for integrity and consistency. This process prevents the restoration of corrupted or compromised data that could lead to further issues.

Data Restoration: Once data integrity is confirmed, the restored data is gradually reintroduced into the vehicle's systems. This process is performed methodically to avoid reinfection or further compromise.

VI. Communication

Internal Communication: Effective internal communication is essential for ensuring all relevant stakeholders are informed about the incident, containment efforts, and recovery steps. This includes notifying engineering teams, security personnel, and relevant departments.

External Communication: Depending on the incident's severity and impact, external communication may be necessary. This can include notifying regulatory bodies, law enforcement, affected customers, and the public if the incident poses a significant risk to safety or privacy.

Media Relations: In some cases, organizations may engage with media relations experts to manage public statements and external communication, ensuring the incident is portrayed accurately and responsibly.

VII. Legal and Regulatory Compliance

Regulatory Reporting: Depending on the location and applicable regulations, organizations may be required to report the incident to regulatory bodies. This is particularly important when the incident involves data breaches or safety-related issues.

Legal Counsel: Legal teams are often engaged to navigate the legal aspects of a cyber incident. They advise on regulatory compliance, potential liabilities, and any legal actions that may be required.

Incident Documentation: Comprehensive documentation of the incident, response efforts, and remediation steps is essential for compliance and any potential legal proceedings.

VIII. Continuous Improvement

Lessons Learned: After the incident, a post-incident review is conducted to analyze the response efforts and identify areas for improvement. Lessons learned from the incident are used to enhance security measures and update incident response plans.

Security Enhancements: The lessons learned are applied to improve security measures, update policies and procedures, and strengthen the organization's overall cybersecurity posture to prevent similar incidents in the future.

Training and Awareness: Regular training and awareness programs are conducted to educate employees and stakeholders about cybersecurity best practices, reducing the likelihood of future incidents.

IX. Incident Simulation and Testing

Tabletop Exercises: Regular tabletop exercises, involving simulated incident scenarios, help response teams practice their response and coordination, identify gaps, and refine the incident response plan.

Red Team Testing: Ethical hackers or red teams are employed to simulate cyberattacks and assess the organization's readiness, detect vulnerabilities, and validate response strategies.

X. Incident Response Automation

Automation Tools: Incident response automation can accelerate detection, containment, and recovery efforts. Automation tools are employed to carry out predefined responses to specific incidents, reducing response time.

AI and Machine Learning: AI and machine learning technologies are employed for more effective and accurate incident detection and analysis, especially in identifying advanced and evolving threats.

Incident Orchestration: Incident response orchestration platforms help streamline and coordinate response efforts, ensuring efficient and consistent actions, which can be particularly valuable in a vehicle's complex electronic systems.

XI. Conclusion

Effective incident response and recovery in the automotive sector are crucial for ensuring the safety, functionality, and data security of connected vehicles. By following these key technical steps and continuously improving incident response strategies, organizations can minimize the impact of incidents, protect their data, and maintain the trust of customers in an era of connected and autonomous vehicles. The evolving threat landscape necessitates a proactive approach to cybersecurity to ensure the integrity and safety of modern vehicles.

Recovery and forensic analysis

Incident response and recovery in the realm of cybersecurity is a multifaceted process that extends beyond containing a breach and eradicating threats. A critical aspect of this process involves recovery and forensic analysis. In this technical discussion, we will delve into the intricate details of these phases, elucidating the methodologies, tools, and techniques employed to restore systems and gather crucial forensic evidence following a cyber incident.

I. Introduction

Recovery and forensic analysis are integral components of the incident response process. While containment and eradication mitigate the immediate threat, recovery focuses on restoring affected systems to their normal state, and forensic analysis aims to uncover the origins, scope, and impact of the incident. These technical aspects are vital for both learning from past incidents and resuming normal operations.

II. Incident Recovery

Backup Restoration: A fundamental step in incident recovery is the restoration of systems and data from secure backups. This ensures that lost data can be retrieved and systems can return to a known, trusted state.

Data Integrity Verification: Before restoring data, it's crucial to verify its integrity. Hash functions and checksums are employed to ensure that restored data has not been tampered with during the incident.

Incremental Recovery: Incremental recovery strategies prioritize critical systems and data, allowing organizations to resume essential operations while conducting a more thorough recovery process.

Network Configuration Reassessment: Network configurations are reassessed to identify and address vulnerabilities or misconfigurations that may have been exploited during the incident.

III. System and Software Patching

Patch Deployment: Identifying and addressing vulnerabilities that contributed to the incident is paramount. Patches, updates, and security fixes are deployed to eliminate the known vulnerabilities.

Software Version Control: Version control ensures that software is up to date and that patched versions are used to replace compromised software.

Testing and Validation: Patch deployment is accompanied by rigorous testing and validation procedures to ensure that the patches do not introduce new issues.

IV. Forensic Analysis

Forensic Image Acquisition: Digital forensic experts acquire forensic images of affected systems and storage media to preserve evidence. Tools like Digital Forensics Framework (DFF) are used for this purpose.

Evidence Chain of Custody: Maintaining a detailed chain of custody is crucial to ensure the admissibility of evidence in legal proceedings. This chain documents who handled the evidence and when.

Memory Analysis: Memory analysis tools like Volatility are employed to examine volatile memory for traces of malicious code, active processes, and indicators of compromise (IOCs).

Log Analysis: Log files from various sources, such as system logs, application logs, and network logs, are meticulously analyzed to reconstruct the timeline of the incident and identify malicious activities.

V. Network Traffic Analysis

Packet Capture: Network traffic packets are captured and analyzed to identify suspicious or malicious network communications. Tools like Wireshark are used for packet analysis.

Flow Analysis: Flow data is analyzed to understand the patterns of network traffic, identifying any deviations from the norm that may indicate a cyber incident.

Intrusion Detection Systems (IDS): IDS logs and alerts are reviewed to identify and trace any detected intrusions, breaches, or malicious activities on the network.

VI. Memory Forensics

Malware Analysis: Memory analysis is crucial for detecting malware that operates in memory, such as fileless malware. Techniques like code injection are examined to identify malicious code.

Process Analysis: Memory analysis tools provide insights into running processes, open network connections, and file system activities within memory.

Artifacts Examination: Forensic analysts scrutinize memory artifacts, including registry hives, event logs, and file handles, to uncover traces of malicious activity.

VII. Disk and File Forensics

File Recovery: Deleted files are often recoverable. Tools like Autopsy and The Sleuth Kit are employed to recover deleted files and analyze their contents.

File Timestamp Analysis: File timestamps, including creation, modification, and access times, are scrutinized to establish when files were accessed or altered during the incident.

File Carving: File carving tools extract files from disk images or unallocated space without relying on file system structures. This is particularly valuable for recovering hidden or deleted data.

VIII. Memory Analysis

Malware Analysis: Memory analysis is crucial for detecting malware that operates in memory, such as fileless malware. Techniques like code injection are examined to identify malicious code.

Process Analysis: Memory analysis tools provide insights into running processes, open network connections, and file system activities within memory.

Artifacts Examination: Forensic analysts scrutinize memory artifacts, including registry hives, event logs, and file handles, to uncover traces of malicious activity.

IX. Disk and File Forensics

File Recovery: Deleted files are often recoverable. Tools like Autopsy and The Sleuth Kit are employed to recover deleted files and analyze their contents.

File Timestamp Analysis: File timestamps, including creation, modification, and access times, are scrutinized to establish when files were accessed or altered during the incident.

File Carving: File carving tools extract files from disk images or unallocated space without relying on file system structures. This is particularly valuable for recovering hidden or deleted data.

X. Data and Artifact Analysis

Registry Analysis: The Windows Registry, a crucial component of Windows operating systems, is analyzed to uncover configuration changes, software installations, and malicious registry entries. Artifact Examination: Artifacts, such as shortcut files, user profiles, and browser histories, are examined to identify user activities and potential indicators of compromise.

Link and Jump List Analysis: Link files and jump lists are scrutinized to understand user interactions, recently accessed files, and applications run during the incident.

XI. Timeline Reconstruction

Event Log Correlation: Correlating event log entries from various sources aids in the reconstruction of a comprehensive timeline of the incident. Tools like log analysis platforms are employed for this purpose.

Attack Chain Analysis: The incident response team analyzes the attack chain, identifying the initial access point, lateral movement, and data exfiltration or tampering to understand the attack's progression.

XII. Report Generation and Documentation

Incident Report: A detailed incident report is generated, documenting all findings, evidence, and actions taken during the forensic analysis process. The report is structured for internal use, legal proceedings, and compliance purposes.

Legal and Regulatory Compliance: The incident report ensures compliance with legal and regulatory requirements, providing the necessary documentation for regulatory bodies and law enforcement.

Lessons Learned: The incident report often includes a section on lessons learned, highlighting areas for improvement and recommendations for enhancing security measures.

XIII. Conclusion

Recovery and forensic analysis are integral to the incident response and recovery process in the realm of cybersecurity. Technical expertise, specialized tools, and meticulous methodologies are crucial for restoring systems to a trusted state, understanding the incident's scope and impact, and preserving evidence for potential legal actions. In the ever-evolving landscape of cyber threats, robust recovery and forensic analysis are essential for enhancing cybersecurity postures and safeguarding organizations from future incidents.

Case Studies

Real-world examples of automotive cyberattacks

In an era of increasingly connected and electronically controlled vehicles, the automotive industry faces growing cybersecurity challenges. Cyberattacks targeting vehicles can have severe consequences, ranging from data theft and privacy breaches to compromising vehicle safety. This technical exploration delves into real-world examples of automotive cyberattacks, shedding light on the methods used, vulnerabilities exploited, and the industry's responses to these threats.

I. Introduction

As vehicles become more sophisticated and connected, the attack surface for cyber threats has expanded. The integration of electronic control units (ECUs), in-vehicle networks, and the connectivity features in modern vehicles has introduced new vulnerabilities. Automotive cyberattacks have gained notoriety due to their potential to endanger lives and compromise sensitive data. This technical discussion will examine actual incidents, dissecting the attack vectors and the subsequent lessons learned by the automotive industry.

II. Case Study 1: The Jeep Cherokee Hack (2015)

Attack Vector: Remote Exploitation through Vulnerable Software

In 2015, security researchers Charlie Miller and Chris Valasek demonstrated the vulnerability of a 2014 Jeep Cherokee by gaining remote control over critical vehicle functions, including steering, acceleration, and braking.

This was made possible through the exploitation of the Uconnect infotainment system's software.

Vulnerabilities Exploited:

- Weaknesses in the Uconnect infotainment system's software, allowing attackers to gain unauthorized access.
- Lack of network segmentation, enabling attackers to pivot from the infotainment system to the vehicle's critical control systems.
- Absence of secure software update mechanisms, enabling remote compromise of the vehicle's software.

Industry Response:

- Fiat Chrysler (the manufacturer of Jeep) issued a recall of 1.4 million vehicles and released a security patch.
- The incident led to increased awareness within the automotive industry regarding the importance of secure software development and over-the-air (OTA) update mechanisms.

III. Case Study 2: Tesla Model S Key Fob Hack (2019)

Attack Vector: Relay Attack Targeting Key Fobs

In 2019, researchers from KU Leuven and the University of Birmingham demonstrated a relay attack that allowed them to steal a Tesla Model S. They intercepted the signals between the vehicle's key fob and the car, tricking the vehicle into unlocking and starting without the key fob being physically present.

Vulnerabilities Exploited:

- Weaknesses in the vehicle's keyless entry system, allowing attackers to relay signals from the key fob over a long distance.

- Lack of secure distance measurement mechanisms in key fob communication.

Industry Response:
- Tesla recommended enabling "PIN to Drive" as an additional layer of security.
- This incident highlighted the importance of secure keyless entry systems and the need for enhanced distance measurement mechanisms in key fobs.

IV. Case Study 3: Mitsubishi Outlander Plug-In Hybrid Hack (2020)

Attack Vector: CAN Bus Manipulation

In 2020, researchers from Pen Test Partners demonstrated a vulnerability in the Mitsubishi Outlander Plug-In Hybrid, which allowed them to disable the vehicle's security system, unlock doors, and start the engine. The attack targeted the vehicle's Controller Area Network (CAN) bus.

Vulnerabilities Exploited:
- Lack of adequate security controls on the CAN bus, allowing unauthorized messages to be sent and received.
- Inadequate authentication and authorization mechanisms within the vehicle's systems.

Industry Response:
- Mitsubishi issued a recall to address the vulnerabilities.
- This incident emphasized the importance of securing the CAN bus and implementing strong authentication and authorization mechanisms.

V. Case Study 4: BMW ConnectedDrive Vulnerabilities (2018)

Attack Vector: Insecure Mobile App and Communication

In 2018, researchers discovered vulnerabilities in the BMW ConnectedDrive platform that allowed attackers to unlock vehicles, manipulate climate control, and access sensitive data. The vulnerabilities were associated with the mobile app used for remote vehicle control.

Vulnerabilities Exploited:

- Weaknesses in the mobile app's authentication mechanisms.
- Inadequate encryption and security controls in the communication between the mobile app and the vehicle.

Industry Response:

- BMW released security updates for its mobile app and improved the encryption of communications.
- This incident emphasized the importance of securing mobile app interfaces and encrypting data in transit.

VI. Case Study 5: Tesla Model X CAN Bus Exploitation (2020)

Attack Vector: CAN Bus Manipulation

In 2020, researchers demonstrated an attack on a Tesla Model X that involved manipulating the vehicle's CAN bus. They gained control over various vehicle functions, including steering, acceleration, and braking.

Vulnerabilities Exploited:

- Weaknesses in the security of the CAN bus, allowing unauthorized messages to be injected.
- Inadequate network segmentation between different vehicle functions.

Industry Response:

- Tesla has made ongoing efforts to improve the security of its vehicles, including implementing hardware-based security mechanisms.
- The incident underscored the need for stringent network segmentation and the protection of critical vehicle functions from external access.

VII. Conclusion

Real-world examples of automotive cyberattacks demonstrate the evolving threat landscape in the automotive industry. As vehicles become more connected and electronically controlled, the importance of cybersecurity measures cannot be overstated. These case studies provide valuable insights into the vulnerabilities exploited by attackers and the responses of automotive manufacturers to address these issues. The automotive industry must continue to invest in cybersecurity measures, secure software development practices, and robust security mechanisms to ensure the safety and security of connected vehicles in the future.

How these attacks were mitigated

In the previous section, we explored real-world examples of automotive cyberattacks that exposed vulnerabilities in modern vehicles. In this technical discussion, we will delve into the strategies and responses used to mitigate these attacks, emphasizing the measures taken by the automotive industry and cybersecurity experts to enhance vehicle security and safeguard against future threats.

I. Introduction

Mitigating automotive cyberattacks is a multifaceted process that involves a combination of preventive, detective, and responsive measures. These measures are aimed at addressing the vulnerabilities exposed in previous cyberattacks and strengthening vehicle security against similar threats.

II. Mitigation of "Company 1" Cyberattack

Response 1: Software Patch and Recall

"Company 1's" response to the cyberattack on its vehicles was swift. They issued a security patch to address the vulnerability in the infotainment system that allowed attackers to gain remote access. Additionally, a recall was initiated to ensure that all affected vehicles received the security update. The security patch mitigated the specific vulnerability used in the attack, rendering the attack vector ineffective.

Response 2: Enhanced Network Segmentation

The cyberattack incident highlighted the need for better network segmentation within vehicles. Manufacturers recognized the importance of isolating critical control systems from less critical systems like infotainment. This enhanced network segmentation helps prevent attackers from pivoting from one system to another.

Response 3: Secure Software Updates

In response to the incident, manufacturers started to focus on the security of software update mechanisms in vehicles. This included implementing secure over-the-air (OTA) update processes that could not be easily exploited by attackers.

III. Mitigation of "Company 2" Cyberattack

Response 1: PIN to Drive

"Company 2's" response to the cyberattack involving key fob relay attacks was to recommend enabling "PIN to Drive." This feature requires the driver to enter a Personal Identification Number (PIN) before the vehicle can be operated. This additional layer of security makes it more difficult for attackers to steal a vehicle through relay attacks.

Response 2: Enhanced Key Fob Security

The cyberattack incident prompted a reevaluation of key fob security. Manufacturers have since focused on developing key fobs with improved distance measurement mechanisms, ensuring that they can only be unlocked and started when they are in close proximity to the vehicle.

IV. Mitigation of "Company 3" Cyberattack

Response 1: Recall and Software Updates

"Company 3's" response to the cyberattack on the Outlander Plug-In Hybrid involved a recall to address the identified vulnerabilities. They released a security patch to eliminate the weaknesses that allowed attackers to disable the vehicle's security system and manipulate vehicle functions.

Response 2: Strengthened CAN Bus Security

The cyberattack incident underscored the importance of securing the Controller Area Network (CAN) bus within vehicles. Manufacturers have since taken measures to improve the security of the CAN bus by implementing authentication and authorization mechanisms and isolating critical vehicle functions from external access.

V. Mitigation of "Company 4" Cyberattack

Response 1: Mobile App Security Updates

"Company 4" responded to the vulnerabilities in its ConnectedDrive platform by releasing security updates for its mobile app. These updates addressed the weaknesses in the mobile app's authentication mechanisms, making it more challenging for attackers to gain unauthorized access.

Response 2: Enhanced Data Encryption

To prevent eavesdropping and man-in-the-middle attacks on communication between the mobile app and the vehicle, "Company 4" improved data encryption. This enhanced the security of data in transit and reduced the risk of data interception.

VI. Mitigation of "Company 5" Cyberattack

Response 1: Hardware-Based Security Mechanisms

"Company 5" has been working on implementing hardware-based security mechanisms within its vehicles. This includes secure gateways and hardware-based encryption to protect critical vehicle systems from unauthorized access.

Response 2: Robust Network Segmentation

The cyberattack incident prompted a reevaluation of network segmentation within "Company 5" vehicles. Stronger network isolation measures have been implemented to prevent attackers from easily moving between different vehicle functions.

VII. Common Mitigation Strategies

Response 1: Security by Design

One of the overarching strategies for mitigating automotive cyberattacks is the principle of "security by design." Manufacturers are increasingly building security into the design and architecture of vehicles from the ground up. This approach involves threat modeling, security assessments, and secure software development practices.

Response 2: Intrusion Detection Systems (IDS)

The implementation of intrusion detection systems within vehicles has become more common. These systems monitor vehicle networks and behavior for signs of suspicious or malicious activities. When an anomaly is detected, the system can take action to block or isolate the threat.

Response 3: Secure Boot Processes

Manufacturers are incorporating secure boot processes to ensure that only trusted and authenticated software can run on a vehicle's electronic control units (ECUs). Secure boot helps prevent the execution of unauthorized or tampered code.

Response 4: Multifactor Authentication (MFA)

MFA is being implemented for systems that require authentication within vehicles. This added layer of security ensures that only authorized users can access critical vehicle functions and settings.

Response 5: Regular Security Updates

Frequent and automatic security updates have become a standard practice. These updates not only address known vulnerabilities but also improve the overall security posture of vehicles by keeping software and firmware up to date.

VIII. Conclusion

The mitigation of automotive cyberattacks is an ongoing and evolving process. The real-world examples of attacks on vehicles have highlighted the vulnerabilities in modern automotive systems, prompting responses from manufacturers and the broader industry. Security measures such as secure software development, network segmentation, intrusion detection systems, and secure boot processes are now fundamental components of vehicle cybersecurity. These strategies aim to not only address past vulnerabilities but also safeguard vehicles against emerging threats, ensuring the safety and security of connected and autonomous vehicles in the future.

Future Trends

The impact of autonomous vehicles

Autonomous vehicles, also known as self-driving cars or driverless vehicles, represent a groundbreaking advancement in transportation technology. These vehicles have the potential to transform the way we travel, offering numerous benefits such as increased safety, improved traffic management, and enhanced mobility for individuals with disabilities. However, the deployment of autonomous vehicles also presents a range of technical challenges and considerations that must be addressed to ensure their successful integration into our transportation systems. This technical exploration delves into the impact of autonomous vehicles, examining their potential benefits, technical components, and the challenges they pose to stakeholders, including manufacturers, regulators, and infrastructure developers.

I. Introduction

Autonomous vehicles are a significant evolution of traditional automobiles. They are equipped with advanced sensors, processors, and software algorithms that allow them to perceive their environment, make informed decisions, and navigate without human intervention. The technical intricacies of autonomous vehicles span a wide range of components and systems, all of which work together to enable safe and efficient autonomous operation.

II. Technical Components of Autonomous Vehicles

> Sensors: Autonomous vehicles rely on a multitude of sensors, including LiDAR (Light Detection and Ranging), radar, cameras, and ultrasonic sensors.

These sensors provide real-time data about the vehicle's surroundings, allowing it to detect and identify objects, pedestrians, road signs, and other vehicles.

Perception Systems: Perception systems process data from sensors to understand the vehicle's environment. Machine learning algorithms analyze sensor data to identify and classify objects, predict their movements, and make decisions based on this information.

Control Systems: Control systems in autonomous vehicles manage steering, acceleration, and braking. They use sensor data and perception system outputs to make split-second decisions and execute vehicle movements.

Mapping and Localization: High-definition maps and GPS data are crucial for autonomous navigation. These maps provide information about road geometry, lane boundaries, and static infrastructure. Localization systems ensure the vehicle knows its precise position on the map.

Connectivity: Autonomous vehicles often rely on V2X (Vehicle-to-Everything) communication, enabling them to communicate with other vehicles, traffic infrastructure, and traffic management systems. This connectivity improves situational awareness and safety.

III. Potential Benefits of Autonomous Vehicles

Improved Safety: Autonomous vehicles have the potential to significantly reduce accidents caused by human error, which is responsible for the majority of traffic incidents. Advanced sensors and real-time data processing allow these vehicles to react faster and make safer decisions.

Enhanced Traffic Management: Autonomous vehicles can communicate with each other and traffic infrastructure to optimize traffic flow, reduce congestion, and decrease travel times.

Increased Mobility for All: Autonomous vehicles can provide greater mobility for individuals with disabilities, the elderly, and those who cannot drive due to medical conditions. They offer a new level of independence and access to transportation.

Fuel Efficiency: Autonomous vehicles can optimize driving patterns and reduce fuel consumption by reducing abrupt stops, optimizing speed, and improving traffic flow.

Reduced Environmental Impact: Autonomous vehicles can contribute to reducing greenhouse gas emissions by promoting efficient driving practices and enabling the use of electric and alternative fuel vehicles.

IV. Technical Challenges and Considerations

Safety and Reliability: Ensuring the safety and reliability of autonomous vehicles is a critical technical challenge. These vehicles must be capable of making split-second decisions to avoid accidents, and their software and hardware components must be rigorously tested for reliability.

Cybersecurity: Autonomous vehicles are susceptible to cyberattacks, which could have life-threatening consequences. Manufacturers must implement robust cybersecurity measures to protect vehicle systems from unauthorized access and manipulation.

Regulatory and Legal Frameworks: The development and deployment of autonomous vehicles require the establishment of clear regulatory and legal frameworks. Technical standards for safety, testing, and data protection must be defined and adhered to.

Data Privacy: Autonomous vehicles generate vast amounts of data, including location information and sensor data. Protecting user privacy and securing this data from potential breaches are significant technical and ethical considerations.

Interoperability and Standardization: To ensure the success of autonomous vehicles, there must be interoperability and standardization of communication protocols and data formats. This facilitates communication between different vehicle models and with existing infrastructure.

V. Infrastructure Considerations

The impact of autonomous vehicles extends beyond the vehicles themselves. Infrastructure development is a critical component of their successful integration. Technical considerations for infrastructure development include:

Sensor Integration: Road infrastructure may need to incorporate sensors and communication equipment to enhance the compatibility of autonomous vehicles with existing infrastructure.

Traffic Management Systems: Traffic management systems must be upgraded to support V2X communication and data sharing with autonomous vehicles. This involves the development of intelligent traffic control systems and real-time traffic data analysis.

Road Markings and Signs: Improving road markings, signs, and traffic signals can enhance the accuracy of vehicle perception systems and facilitate navigation.

Charging and Refueling Infrastructure: Autonomous electric and alternative-fuel vehicles require convenient and efficient charging or refueling infrastructure. Developing such infrastructure is a technical challenge in itself.

VI. Conclusion

The impact of autonomous vehicles on our society, economy, and daily lives is profound. The technical components that enable these vehicles to operate autonomously are complex and interdependent. While they offer numerous benefits such as improved safety, enhanced traffic management, and increased mobility, they also present significant technical challenges related to safety, reliability, cybersecurity, and data privacy. Addressing these challenges and coordinating technical advancements with regulatory frameworks and infrastructure development will be essential to unlock the full potential of autonomous vehicles and shape the future of transportation.

Emerging cybersecurity technologies and challenges

The field of cybersecurity is in a perpetual state of evolution as it grapples with the relentless advancements in technology and the ever-growing threat landscape. As organizations and individuals become more reliant on digital systems, the need for cutting-edge cybersecurity technologies and practices is more critical than ever. This technical exploration delves into emerging cybersecurity technologies and the challenges that they aim to address, emphasizing the technical aspects that underpin these developments.

I. Introduction

Cybersecurity is a multidisciplinary field that encompasses a vast array of technologies, strategies, and practices. As the digital world continues to expand and evolve, new challenges and threats constantly emerge, necessitating the development and implementation of innovative cybersecurity solutions. In this exploration, we will delve into emerging cybersecurity technologies, their technical intricacies, and the challenges they seek to confront.

II. Emerging Cybersecurity Technologies

Artificial Intelligence (AI) and Machine Learning (ML): AI and ML are at the forefront of cybersecurity. These technologies enable the development of advanced threat detection, anomaly identification, and predictive analysis systems. They can analyze vast datasets and identify patterns that human operators might miss.

Zero Trust Architecture: Zero Trust is a security model that treats every user and device as potentially untrusted, regardless of their location within or outside the corporate network. It emphasizes the principle of "never trust, always verify" and relies on strict identity verification and continuous monitoring.

Quantum-Safe Cryptography: As quantum computing advances, it threatens traditional cryptographic systems. Quantum-safe or post-quantum cryptography aims to develop algorithms and encryption methods that are resistant to quantum attacks.

Container and Cloud Security: With the proliferation of containerization and cloud computing, security solutions tailored to these environments are crucial. Technologies like runtime protection, container security scanning, and cloud access security brokers (CASBs) are emerging.

Blockchain for Security: Blockchain, known for its role in cryptocurrencies, is also being explored for cybersecurity applications. It can enhance data integrity, secure authentication, and create transparent and immutable logs.

Behavioral Biometrics: Behavioral biometrics analyze user behavior, such as typing patterns, mouse movements, and touchscreen interactions, to verify user identity. It provides an additional layer of security beyond traditional authentication methods.

Deception Technologies: Deception technologies involve setting up decoy systems, data, or assets to mislead and detect attackers. When adversaries interact with these decoys, security teams gain insight into their tactics and intent.

III. Technical Challenges in Emerging Cybersecurity

AI and ML Trustworthiness: AI and ML models are susceptible to adversarial attacks, where attackers manipulate data to deceive machine learning algorithms. Ensuring the trustworthiness and resilience of AI and ML systems is a significant technical challenge.

Zero Trust Implementation: Implementing a Zero Trust architecture can be technically complex, especially in large organizations with legacy systems. It requires the development of robust identity verification and access control mechanisms.

Quantum-Resistant Cryptography: Developing and deploying cryptographic systems that are quantum-resistant is a formidable technical challenge. These systems must be secure against both classical and quantum attacks.

Container and Cloud Security Integration: Ensuring that security solutions seamlessly integrate with container and cloud environments, while maintaining visibility and control, is a technical challenge. It requires careful orchestration of security tools.

Blockchain Scalability: Blockchain technologies face scalability challenges, especially in public networks. To be viable for cybersecurity applications, blockchain must overcome technical barriers related to speed, cost, and resource consumption.

Behavioral Biometrics Accuracy: Behavioral biometrics rely on accurately recognizing and distinguishing user behavior patterns. Achieving high accuracy and preventing false positives or negatives is a technical challenge that requires continuous refinement.

Deception Technology Realism: Deception technologies must be convincingly realistic to deceive attackers effectively. Achieving this level of realism while ensuring scalability and minimal impact on legitimate users is a technical challenge.

IV. Technical Collaboration and Research

Emerging cybersecurity technologies require collaborative research efforts among academia, industry, and government agencies. Addressing these technical challenges often involves developing new algorithms, protocols, and security mechanisms. Ensuring interoperability and standardized practices is essential.

V. Regulatory and Ethical Considerations

The deployment of emerging cybersecurity technologies is not only a technical challenge but also a legal and ethical one. Regulations and ethical considerations around data privacy, user consent, and responsible AI usage are critical aspects of the cybersecurity landscape.

VI. Conclusion

As the digital world continues to evolve, the technical challenges and complexities in the realm of cybersecurity grow in tandem. Emerging technologies, while promising enhanced security, also introduce new vulnerabilities and attack vectors. Addressing these challenges requires a combination of technical innovation, collaboration, and a commitment to maintaining the confidentiality, integrity, and availability of digital systems in an ever-changing threat landscape. It is through these efforts that we can stay one step ahead of cyber adversaries and ensure the ongoing security of our digital ecosystems.

Conclusion and Final Thoughts

The ongoing importance of automotive cybersecurity

In an era where the lines between the physical and digital worlds are increasingly blurred, the automotive industry finds itself at the crossroads of an unprecedented transformation. The once mechanical heart of vehicles has been infused with a digital soul, driving innovations that promise to revolutionize how we perceive and interact with transportation. From connected cars that communicate with the world around them to autonomous vehicles poised to redefine our very relationship with driving, the automotive landscape has undergone a remarkable metamorphosis.

However, with great promise comes the inevitability of great responsibility. As vehicles evolve into complex digital ecosystems, automotive cybersecurity has emerged as a critical imperative. The importance of safeguarding these digital conduits, which impact not only our daily lives but also our safety, privacy, and the very fabric of our society, cannot be overstated. In this extensive technical conclusion, we reflect on the journey through the multifaceted world of automotive cybersecurity, delving into its enduring importance and the need for continual vigilance and innovation in the face of evolving threats.

I. The Shifting Paradigm of the Automotive Industry

The automotive industry stands at the cusp of a new era, a renaissance of sorts, where traditional notions of vehicles are being redefined and reimagined. The shift towards connected and autonomous vehicles represents the zenith of this transformation. These vehicles, infused with cutting-edge technology, have the potential to enhance safety, revolutionize transportation, and significantly reduce environmental impact. They bring with them the promise of a future where traffic accidents are virtually eliminated, mobility is accessible to all, and driving is no longer bound by human limitations.

Yet, beneath the surface of this profound transformation lies a paradox—the intersection of boundless possibilities and unparalleled vulnerability. As vehicles become increasingly digital and interconnected, they are no longer confined to the physical world; they are as much a part of the digital realm. This paradigm shift raises questions about the security, integrity, and trustworthiness of these vehicles, making automotive cybersecurity an imperative.

II. The Ongoing Importance of Automotive Cybersecurity

The importance of automotive cybersecurity is underpinned by a host of compelling factors that ensure its enduring relevance:

> Connected and Autonomous Vehicles: The emergence of connected and autonomous vehicles is a testament to human ingenuity. However, these technological marvels are highly dependent on software and communication networks. While they bring us closer to the vision of autonomous driving, they also expose us to an expanded attack surface, making them susceptible to cyber threats. Ensuring the security and integrity of these systems is an inescapable responsibility.

> Safety and Liability: As we move towards a future with fully autonomous vehicles, questions of liability become paramount. In the event of a cyber-related accident, who is to blame? Is it the vehicle owner, the software developer, or a malicious attacker?

Automotive cybersecurity is not merely about protecting data; it is about safeguarding lives, and this critical dimension cannot be overlooked.

Consumer Trust: Trust is the cornerstone of the automotive industry. If consumers do not trust the security of their vehicles, they may be hesitant to adopt new technologies. Ensuring the security of vehicles is not only a matter of technical competence but also a reflection of an automaker's commitment to the well-being of its customers.

Data Privacy: The data generated by modern vehicles is a treasure trove of insights. From driving behavior to location information, this data can provide valuable services and improve user experiences. However, the sheer volume and sensitivity of this data demand robust security and privacy measures. Protecting user data from unauthorized access and ensuring its responsible use are critical aspects of automotive cybersecurity.

Regulatory Scrutiny: Governments and regulatory bodies around the world are closely scrutinizing the cybersecurity of vehicles. They are developing standards and regulations aimed at enforcing cybersecurity practices across the industry. Compliance with these regulations is not a choice but an obligation.

Evolving Threat Landscape: Cyber threats are not static; they continually evolve. As cybercriminals become more sophisticated and determined, new vulnerabilities and attack vectors emerge. The automotive industry must not only contend with known threats but also anticipate and prepare for the unknown. Staying ahead of these threats is a perpetual challenge.

III. The Future of Automotive Cybersecurity

As we traverse the uncharted territory of automotive cybersecurity, it is imperative to consider the path forward. The future of automotive cybersecurity hinges on several key considerations:

Education and Training: Cybersecurity is not just a technical field; it is a cultural and organizational shift. Developing a workforce that is cybersecurity-aware is crucial. Engineers, developers, and all those involved in automotive design and manufacturing need to be well-versed in cybersecurity principles. Education and training programs that cultivate a security-conscious mindset are essential.

Security by Design: It is no longer acceptable to consider cybersecurity as an afterthought. Vehicles must be designed with security in mind from the very beginning. This design ethos spans the entire lifecycle of the vehicle, from the initial concept to development, testing, and deployment.

Collaboration and Information Sharing: No single entity can stand alone against the dynamic and multifaceted threat landscape. The automotive industry must foster a culture of collaboration and information sharing. Threat intelligence sharing and collaboration with cybersecurity experts, organizations, and government agencies are vital to anticipate and counteract threats.

Regulatory Compliance: Adherence to automotive cybersecurity regulations and standards is not only a legal requirement but a moral obligation. Manufacturers and stakeholders must remain informed about evolving legal and regulatory obligations and ensure compliance. The development and maintenance of security standards, guidelines, and best practices are intrinsic to this compliance.

Threat Modeling and Risk Assessment: Comprehensive threat modeling and risk assessments must become routine practice in the automotive industry. By assessing and identifying vulnerabilities and potential risks, manufacturers and cybersecurity experts can prioritize security measures and implement them effectively.

Security Testing and Validation: Rigorous security testing is paramount. Penetration testing, vulnerability assessments, and ethical hacking practices are crucial to identifying and rectifying vulnerabilities in vehicles. The implementation of robust security protocols, as well as the monitoring and maintenance of these protocols, are fundamental to secure vehicle operation.

Continual Innovation: Cyber threats are not static, nor should cybersecurity be. Advancements in technology must be met with equal or superior advancements in security. New challenges will arise, and the automotive industry must demonstrate its capacity for innovation in the face of these challenges.

IV. A Journey into the Digital Age

The ongoing importance of automotive cybersecurity is not a burden; it is an imperative, a fundamental duty. It safeguards lives, data, and the future of transportation. While the landscape is complex and ever-changing, the principles that guide automotive cybersecurity remain unwavering: vigilance, education, collaboration, and innovation. As we journey further into an era of connected and autonomous vehicles, let us navigate this road with unwavering dedication to automotive cybersecurity.

The road ahead is filled with opportunities for innovation and challenges that demand collective vigilance and dedication. It is a journey into the digital age where every advancement is an invitation for further exploration, learning, and innovation. It is a journey where automotive cybersecurity stands as a stalwart guardian, ensuring that our vehicles remain safe, secure, and resilient against the ever-present threats of the digital age.

This journey is not one of isolation but of collaboration. It is a journey where automotive manufacturers, cybersecurity experts, regulatory bodies, and individuals stand together, recognizing that the responsibility of ensuring automotive cybersecurity is a shared one. It is a journey where the destination is not merely a place but a vision—a vision of a future where vehicles are not just modes of transportation but beacons of trust, safety, and innovation.

In this digital odyssey, automotive cybersecurity will continue to play a pivotal role, evolving, adapting, and growing stronger with each step. It will not just be a guardian; it will be an enabler, empowering us to embrace the boundless opportunities of the digital age while protecting what matters most—our lives, our data, and our journey into an exciting and uncertain future. It is a journey that has just begun, and as we move forward, the enduring importance of automotive cybersecurity will light our way.